A DOCTOR AT WAR

The story of
Colonel Martin Herford
The most decorated
doctor of
World War Two

A DOCTOR AT
WAR

The story of
Colonel Martin Herford
The most decorated
doctor of
World War Two

MATTHEW HALL

IMAGES
PUBLISHING

First published in Great Britain 1995 by
Images Publishing (Malvern) Ltd.,
The Wells House, Holywell Road, Malvern Wells,
Worcestershire WR14 4LH

British Library Cataloguing in Publication Data

A catalogue record for this book is available
from the British Library

ISBN 1 897817 54 1

Cover photograph of ambulance taken by
Lieut Murray and Sgts R H Morris and Muir.
Crown Copyright Imperial War Museum, London

Designed and Produced by Images Publishing (Malvern) Ltd.
Printed and Bound in Great Britain by Bookcraft, Bath, Avon.

C O N T E N T S

for
Patricia and Thomas

PROLOGUE

The Second World War claimed the lives of forty-six million soldiers and civilians, making it the greatest ever catastrophe to befall mankind. Were it not for the efforts of the thousands of Medical Officers and staff who accompanied the Allied armies throughout battles across three continents, the fatalities would undoubtedly have been far higher. More often than not historians have tended to ignore this vital part of the Forces, no doubt because military doctors tend not to become directly involved in combat. But that is not to say that they did not often find themselves in the front line; the popular image of a team of medics tucked safely away in a hospital tent well behind lines is a gross misrepresentation. The doctors and stretcher bearers had the job of plucking casualties from the battle field while bullets were still flying and shells exploding, and coolly ensuring that treatment was given in casualty clearing stations no matter what was happening outside.

The aim of this book is to give a simple account of a single soldier, Dr Martin Herford, who became one of the most decorated front-line British doctors of World War II. The author's intention has not been to write a eulogy; there are thousands of unsung heroes who will never have the privilege of having a biography written about them. Rather, it has been to give an insight into one man's unique experience of a war which took him through Spain, Finland, North Africa, Greece, Sicily, Italy, Normandy, and finally to the liberation of Belsen concentration camp; and to let it stand as an example of the experiences of others like him, who, in the many perilous situations which confronted them, learned to live with the threat of death in the pursuit of saving life.

When it comes to discussing his own achievements, Dr Herford

11

has proved to be a modest man – reserve typical of the wartime generation, who were imbued from an early age with a distaste for self aggrandisement. It is also perhaps due to the soldier's natural reaction to the horrors of war, which is to develop an efficient exterior in which emotion is allowed to play little or no part. But the unembellished facts of Dr Herford's achievements, and those of his colleagues, pieced together from recollections, diaries, and a prolific correspondence, speak for themselves.

CHAPTER 1

The Formative Years

In 1905 on the Himalayan foothills above the North Indian town of Srinagar, Dr Ethilda Meakin was travelling alone with a party of twelve Indian servants for a well deserved vacation in one of the dak bungalows frequented by the ex-patriot population as a holiday location. She had come to India three years earlier to preside over the Zanana Mission women's hospital in Bombay, and had subsequently been appointed to the women's hospital in Calcutta. The need for women doctors in India's over crowded hospitals was acute, as religious customs largely forbade native women from being examined by male doctors. But despite her robust Victorian constitution, the dust, flies and disease of the city could not be endured for months on end without occasional periods of relaxation. The sea voyage to England could take up to six weeks, so for those who could not spare the time, the next best thing was a vacation in the beautiful and refreshing mountains of the north.

On her way up the hill sides that summer she encountered another tough and enterprising individual, Oscar Haarbleicher, a partner in the Calcutta-based company Allen Brothers, Importers Agents. The two of them struck up a friendship and soon became the subject of idle gossip amongst the well-heeled ex-patriots. The holiday meeting did not initially develop into romance, and the couple confined their intimacy to playing lengthy games of chess and walking together, but the English ladies would not let the opportunity of creating a successful match pass by – Ethilda was already in her early thirties, and Oscar several years older, both past the usual marriageable age. Over the coming months the two were thrown together at a succession of Calcutta social events. Close friends even bought wedding presents in anticipation of their engagement being announced; but it was two years before Oscar finally proposed, and several more months before they were married in Calcutta Cathedral.

By any standards, Ethilda was an exceptional woman, highly educated, fearless and with an enquiring spirit – qualities she shared with other members of her family. Her father Edward Meakin was a leading expert in the history of Morocco who had previously set up the first English language newspaper in Morocco, the *Morocco Times*. Ethilda's brother Harold, a graduate of Barts, had commanded the medical contingent sent to the relief of the troops in Peking during the Opium Wars. Her sister Mary was the first Western woman to travel accross the Trans Siberian railway and wrote numerous books and translations of Göethe and Schiller.

Also related (her maternal grandfather) was Samuel Budgett, the 'Successful Merchant', whose bust still stands on the stairs of Bristol City Museum. A pioneer of industrial reform in the employment of labour and a colleague of Shaftesbury and Carnegie, his achievements are recorded in two immensely popular books of the time, *Men Who Win* by William Thegar and *The Successful Merchant* by William Arthur. Each of these sold many thousands of copies in Britain and American, and went through 22 editions, a rarity at that time.

Ethilda herself had wanted to become a doctor from early childhood, much to the alarm of her parents, who, despite their adventurous lifestyle, held conventional ambitions for their daughter. In a bid to try to crush her zeal they arranged a trip for her to perform good works with a charity in 'Gorbals', one of the filthy tenements in Glasgow, when she was in her late teens. To their surprise she went willingly, and there had her first real exposure to poverty, disease and deprivation; but this only served to strengthen her resolve, and in due course she won a place at the Royal Free Hospital, later qualifying as one of only eight female graduates in 1898.

one of only eight female graduates in 1898.

Once qualified, Ethilda also developed an intense interest in the fledgling science of psychoanalysis, and particularly in the writings of Farenzi and Freud. In 1909, with her first child Harold still a toddler, she decided to stop in Geneva to attend a conference at which Freud was a principal speaker, on her way back from Calcutta for a period of leave in England. By the time the ship arrived in Marseilles, she was nearly nine months pregnant with her second child. Oscar had remained in India, and the prospect of crossing France by train with the danger of the onset of labour cannot have been attractive. But from Marseilles she cabled to her sister-in-law in England, asking her to join her in Switzerland. Undaunted, she travelled on alone to Geneva where she managed to give birth to a second son, Martin, in time to attend the conference!

Oscar followed his wife to England where they remained until 1913. In 1912 they had a third child, this time a daughter, Sylvia, who was also to grow up to become a doctor.

Martin spent the first four years of his life in Brighton. He became extremely close to his elder brother Harold, on whom he relied heavily as the two grew older and went to school together. To them, their mother was a relaxed, carefree figure who loved the open air and doted on her children; their father a somewhat stern Victorian gentleman. Although Oscar may have had a harsh exterior, he had a passionate interest in music and was an accomplished violinist. He desperately wanted his children to be musical, but the overbearing manner of his instruction only managed to frighten them, for whenever they sat at the piano they knew that any wrong notes would be met with a loud bellow, even from the top of the house.

In 1913 Oscar had to return to India for six months on business. Ethilda did not want to be separated from him, but decided to bring only the baby with her. This was nothing unusual as it was common practice for couples to leave their children with friends and relatives whilst they remained out of the country, both as an assurance against disease, and to give their offspring the benefit of an English education. A baby could not of course be left without its mother, but caring for it in India could be a hazardous business. Even in houses with staff, hygiene was poor unless the servants were very carefully instructed, and the common method adopted by servant women to quieten a crying baby was to scratch up some opium under the finger nail and give the baby the finger to suck.

Although Ethilda and Oscar's intentions for their two sons were entirely honourable, the manner of their departure was, by modern standards, traumatic. The two boys were taken by their parents to a house called Travishes on the outskirts of Exeter, run by Mrs Sweet, a lady who took in the children of parents who were in India. When they arrived Martin and Harold were introduced to some of the other children and told they were going to live with them. In the unquestioning way of a four-year-old, Martin happily ran out with them to look at the garden, excited at the prospect of having some new companions. But on his return he found that his parents had disappeared without trace. Fortunately Harold seemed to have had the situation explained to him, and was able to reassure his distressed younger brother, who was feeling desolate.

Had Oscar had any idea of the political events which were to follow, he would surely have abandoned his trip or taken his sons with them. With the outbreak of war shipping from India was severely restricted, and Oscar and Ethilda did not see their sons again until 1917.

At first the boys were happy in the house in Exeter. With the help of her two daughters, Mrs Sweet was mostly very kind, but on occasions the boys clearly tried her patience. In a letter to their father dated 22 September 1915 she wrote:

'The fact is that my daughters and I have been feeling for some time that Harold and Martin are beginning to require more strict supervision than we can give them. Whether it is due to neglect of training in their babyhood, and the constant absences of their mother, or from whatever other cause, their whole idea seems to be how they can take people in. They tell long stories of the French nurse who used to take in their mother so cleverly, so I think she must have a great deal to do with it . . . I feel sure that under the strict guidance of a <u>man</u> at the head of things they will improve with <u>time</u>, but nothing else will do. Of that I feel sure, and nothing could be worse for the training of the two younger children than to be brought up with their brothers until they have learned from a man that it is unmannerly to tell a lie or to pilfer things that do not belong to them.'

Despite these outbursts, the boys enjoyed their time with Mrs Sweet, and were often visited by relatives and friends of their parents, one of whom treated them to a memorable outing in a motor car – a rare and exquisite pleasure for small boys at that time. However, this relatively happy situation was brought to an abrupt end when Mrs Sweet's only son, a Padre in the Royal Navy, was killed when his ship struck a German mine in Portsmount harbour. Although she had cared for Martin and Harold with the same affection she showed towards the other children, despite their German surname, visitors to the house constantly commented that it was not right for her to be looking after two young 'Germans'. Finally she felt that she had no choice but to turn them out, and arrangements were made for them to go and live with a blind lady and her sister in Ilfracombe.

Such was the level of anti-German feeling, that Oscar changed the family name to Herford shortly after war broke out – a business colleague told him squarely that no Englishman would do business

17

with a man with a German name. The sacrifice of his name was particularly upsetting to Oscar as in 1848 his grandfather, a prominent German Jew in Hamburg, had sent his two sons out of the country, one to Manchester and one to Paris, declaring that Germany under Bismark was 'no place for a free man.' England during the Great War was obviously no place for a free German.

Martin and Harold's experiences in Ilfracombe were not so happy. An old-fashioned governess called Miss Bobers was employed to look after them, and her antiquated methods of correcting misbehaviour go a long way to explaining why a generation of middle class children grew up plagued with guilt and an inability to express their stifled emotions. Martin, being the younger and more temperamental of the two, was prone to tantrums and fits of tears. Miss Bobers' 'cure' was to make him walk through the streets with a notice attached to his back declaring, 'I must not be a cry-baby.' Even more cruelly, if the upset child wet his bed, which he frequently did, he was forced to parade with another notice reading, 'I must not be a bed-wetter.' Thankfully, one day when Miss Bobers was accompanying Martin on one of his walks of shame a passer-by stopped and gave her a stern lecture. She was evidently shamed into submission herself, as the indignity was never repeated.

It would be wrong to pass over this incident without remarking that Miss Bobers was probably not a wicked woman, but was merely carrying out what she had been taught – that only by shaming the child into recognising his faults would he overcome them and grow in character. This view is reinforced by the fact that there is no suggestion that the boys were beaten or mistreated in any other way.

The shipping lanes to the East were finally reopened in 1917, and Ethilda and Oscar immediately returned to their sons. By this time they had a fourth child, George. The usual practice in wartime was for husbands and wives to travel on different ships as accidents were a relatively frequent occurrence on seas littered with mines. Ethilda returned first with the two children without incident. Oscar followed on another ship with all the family furniture and possessions. Disaster struck when the ship hit a mine just off Marseilles. He was saved, but all their belongings were lost.

Although every stick of furniture and shred of clothing had gone down with the ship, Oscar thankfully had sufficient money to buy a house in Reading. He was by now forty-eight years old and his firm had done well. He had a substantial amount of capital still invested with them, and expected a handsome return. Happy as he was to be reunited with his sons, the boys took some time to readjust to family life, and for some time were very disobedient. It took their parents several painful months to win back their trust and confidence.

Ethilda was determined above all else that her children, including Sylvia, would receive the best education they could afford. When her daughter was still only two weeks old, she had visited Miss Lawrence, an old friend and the Headmistress of Roedean school, and asked that her daughter's name be put down. Latterly, educating the children involved great sacrifice as in 1925 Oscar suffered a financial disaster. His former colleagues in India had risked his money in a series of ill-advised and highly speculative investments that came to nothing. Instead of being reasonably affluent as he had expected, he found himself in his mid-fifties virtually penniless. He was reduced to approaching charities for help with school expenses, and Ethilda worked as a schools medical officer.

Martin and Harold were first sent away to school to Marlborough House, near Reading. Martin's time there was not happy. He was small, although physically able to hold his own in most sports, and never easily fitted in with the other boys; because of his size, they treated him more like a mascot than one of the gang. Luckily he was very independent, and never minded to obey authority merely for the sake of it or to look for approval from his peers. These were qualities which were to distinguish him in later life, but which in the environment of a public school inevitably led to conflict.

The Headmaster of Marlborough House was an unhappy bachelor who lived with an ageing mother. He took out his frustrations on the boys by caning them with a fervour bordering on sadism. His favourite trick for singling out victims was to creep along the boarding house corridors late at night in stockinged feet, listening for boys talking; any boy who was heard would be called to his study the next morning for a severe beating. Any little fault in the class room or misbehaviour in the playground was similarly rewarded, either with a sharp whack on the palm of the hand or with several painful strokes across the buttocks, which made sitting down very uncomfortable.

Martin was greatly relieved when, the following year, he and Harold became day pupils and cycled into school. But the frequent beatings didn't abate, and the Headmaster's excuses for punishing the young Herford became ever more tenuous. On one occasion during a French lesson, the young French master was showing the class his brother's revolver which had been struck by shrapnel in the Somme and saved his life. The boys chattered excitedly as they heard the tale, attracting the attention of the Headmaster who was passing along the corridor. He burst into the classroom and accused Martin of having made the noise. Despite the protests of the young Master, Martin was dragged off to the Head's study and told to bend over. Martin refused and broke two of his canes before eventually being thrown to the floor and given a double thrashing. Despite the sharp, slicing pain, Martin yelled out 'Oh, sah! Oh, sah!' in a successful attempt to embarrass his tormentor.

The next day, he feigned illness and refused to get out of bed, certain that another beating was waiting for him at school. Eventually his mystified parents managed to drag the truth out of him and packed him off to school with a letter addressed to the Headmaster. Miraculously, he wasn't caned again.

Worried by the overly punitive regime at Marlborough House, which had only served to instil in Martin a deep-seated mistrust for authority bordering on contempt, and concerned that Martin was becoming too dependent on his elder brother, his parents decided to send them to different schools at the start of the following term. Harold went to Wellington, a public school with strong military connections. He was not academically gifted, but in the physically rigorous environment of Wellington he would be able to hold his own. Martin, still only ten years old, was sent as a boarder to a small school at Bembridge on the Isle of Wight, recently formed by a group of Friends. Ethilda's enduring interest in education led her later to become one of its school governors.

Martin could not have hoped for a freer and more relaxed environment. The school was in a perfect position, situated opposite the steep, sloping Culver cliffs and looking out to sea. Outside lessons, the boys were free to scramble across the muddy cliffs and along the shore. They built dens in the dense masses of blackthorn bushes that grew behind the beaches, and formed themselves into opposing 'gangs', pelting each other with hard, sun-baked clay missiles and using dustbin lids 'borrowed' from neighbouring houses as shields. They made themselves thoroughly unpopular with some of the local residents, but enjoyed an almost blissful outdoor existence.

The school's liberal approach was extremely forward-looking for its time, and without the oppression of stifling authority Martin began to grow more self assured. For the first time he began to read with great enthusiasm: there was even a joke amongst his friends that he managed to read under the shower. He was still small for his age, but Martin took to swimming, climbing on the cliffs and was as good as any of his contemporaries and many of the older boys on the tennis court, even though he had to manage with his father's heavy, old fashioned racquet.

Success in individual sports did nothing to remedy the fact that by temperament he was not a team player. In later years Herford said that as a schoolboy he had a dislike of being in the lead. This may have been borne of a lack of self confidence, or of the awe in which he held his older brother. It may simply have been due to the fact that he was a relatively immature adolescent who was more than usually sensitive to the jibes of others. Whatever the reason, he remained a relative outsider throughout his school career. His favourite pastimes were always solitary, and on moonlit summer nights he would sneak from the boarding house and walk down alone to the sea, either to fish for bass or just to watch the moonlight dancing on the water. These two brief years at Bembridge were among the happiest of his life.

The end of 'prep' school signalled a return to Berkshire. This time, Martin was sent to Leighton Park school near Reading. His parents considered that he must live his school life to the full, so he was sent as a boarder, even though his home was less than half a mile away. Leighton Park was a Quaker school, attended by the sons of wealthy Quaker businessmen. Early Quakers were barred from joining the professions so they therefore became merchants, and often very successful and philanthropic ones with pioneering labour relations policies.

Success in business in turn brought with it social acceptance in the 'best circles'. When Martin arrived at Leighton Park one of a group of boys asked him whether he was related to the Duke of Hereford. When he replied that he wasn't, he was immediately marked down as of little social significance and not useful to know. As one Headmaster later wrote, this era was the 'nadir' of the school. The boys formed into tight impenetrable cliques, creating an unhealthy and often hostile atmosphere. For a natural loner like Martin, widespread acceptance by the others was almost an impossibility. He was not the subject of physical bullying, but he remained isolated and on the edge of the groups.

His unhappiness at school was heightened by the financial difficulties at home. While the other boys were dressed in fine new clothes, Martin's were worn and threadbare.

Martin took himself out of his troubles by developing an intense interest in another solitary pastime, ornithology. Leighton Park's greatest asset was its one hundred acres of fine grounds, which boasted a rich and varied selection of wildlife. The Headmaster, himself a keen ornithologist, allowed Martin to get up before dawn and go out with his binoculars to watch for the arrival of the spring migrants. To the Headmaster this was no more than an innocent hobby, but already Martin was possessed of enormous self discipline and an unswerving ability to pursue his own course despite the opinions of those around him. There was very little self pity about the child, who seemed always to accept his current situation and succeed in turning it to his advantage.

On his sixteenth birthday, Martin took the school matriculation, and unfortunately failed in one subject, chemistry. For a boy who was obviously bright and who was later to become a doctor it was an unexpected result, although of a class of sixteen, only one did pass the exam. Martin's parents, who had made great sacrifices to pay his fees, simply could not afford to keep him at Leighton Park any longer. Instead, he went for the autumn term to Reading School where he sat the External Matric. To his parents great relief, this time he passed.

Although the Quakers were ideological pacifists, Martin did not feel particularly bound by their injunctions or indeed by any political or religious creed; but he had made up his mind by his mid-teens that he was not capable of killing another human being. The accounts he had read of the mass slaughter in the Great War had made a profound impression, and helped formulate his ambition to follow his mother into medicine. It was the only profession in which he felt he could be of any real use to humanity.

In the 1920s grants for university education were hard to obtain.

Studying medicine meant many expensive years which his parents simply could not afford, so Martin opted to apply for a BSc course at Reading University. Studying there would allow him to remain living at home, and also to be with his beloved brother Harold, who was already there reading Agriculture.

In the intervening ten months Martin was sent to stay with his German uncle and his family, the Haarbleichers, in Hamburg, for the express purpose of learning the language. Hampered initially by a reticence to speak at all, his hosts began to view him as almost retarded! But he was thrown in at the deep end and made to attend a German school with his cousins. Gradually he began to pick up some ungrammatical but functional German.

At that time Germany was suffering badly from economic recession and the after-effects of the Versailles Treaty. There was much popular bitterness directed towards the more affluent Jewish communities, amongst whom numbered Herford's relations. The Haarbleichers were of Jewish descent, although no longer practising. There was talk at the dinner table of the rise of anti-Jewish sentiment, but in the 1920s there was still no hint of the horrors which were to follow. Martin was for the most part unaware of these undercurrents, and began to throw himself into the family life of his cousins.

After the summer term each year, pupils were sent on extended trips to different parts of the country. The idea was to familiarise them with all parts of their nation, and to implant a degree of independence from the family. The children were moved around in railway trucks, sometimes with only straw over the bare boards to sit and sleep on, but it was a time of great excitement, and the children loved it. Martin and his cousins stayed in a number of youth hostels – an institution as yet unknown in Britain – and roamed the countryside.

This informal introduction to Germany and its people was an invaluable experience. Apart from learning the language, Martin also gained a vital insight into the German temperament. When, during the war, he was called upon to cross enemy lines under the Red Cross flag, he could do so with a certain amount of faith that the men he would meet on the other side were not all evil snarling monsters who would shoot him down with disregard for the rules of warfare. He learned, that, for ordinary Germans at least, the concept of honour was paramount. The average German would no more debase himself through a needlessly callous act than an Englishman. It was therefore with great sadness and with a great deal of affection for the generous and welcoming people who had welcomed him into their homes, that Martin left Hamburg to start his degree course in Reading.

The general science degree upon which he embarked did not fill him with ambition and enthusiasm. He and his brother Harold stuck close together and in preference to their studies spent a relatively carefree year fishing, bird watching and playing tennis. Harold passed his examinations in agriculture, but Martin had studied so little that it was not even worthwhile for him to sit the intermediate science paper.

Soon after completing his studies Harold enthusiastically accepted an offer from a friend of his father's to take up a position on a sugar estate in India. Harold leapt at the chance, thrilled at the prospect of the shooting and pig-sticking – 'sports' which Martin found abhorrent – and left England with few regrets. Martin, on the other hand, was at a loose end. An old friend of his mother's, his Godmother, for whom he had great respect, was prepared to help finance him to study law as she was married to a barrister and enjoyed a comfortable living, but Martin was not attracted by the prospect. Eventually his father took the initiative and found him a job in Pulsometer, an engineering firm in Reading.

Martin spent four years working in a company which held little interest for him. It was a period of his life during which he had neither drive, nor a particular desire to achieve anything. He was trained in every department of the company and became secretary to the Managing Director, but he felt stifled, and soon realised that he would rather be working on a banana plantation in some far flung corner of the Empire rather than be stuck in a factory.

With encouragement from an aunt (a Founder of the Women's Police and responsible for their training), who agreed to help him financially, and also from his mother, Martin eventually managed to secure a place to study medicine at Bristol university, which he chose for the simple reason that his younger brother had already gone to work for Robinsons, a firm which had its Headquarters there.

The five years in Bristol were happy ones. Martin and George, his younger brother, shared a small flat, with a spare bedroom where a friend could stay, and enjoyed a simple lifestyle. As well as studying hard, Martin played a lot of sport, eventually playing hockey for Gloucester County and the Combined Universities. He became captain of Tennis and Badminton, and ran the mile for the university in 1936. Vacations were often spent walking in the Lake District or on the Yorkshire Moors. Evidencing considerable physical stamina, Martin made his journeys across country by bicycle or on foot, cycling over 150 miles in a day, carrying camping kit of 40-50 lb., sleeping in a small tent, many miles from human habitation.

Whilst at Bristol Martin and George became very close. George, a thoughtful, quiet lad, in common with both his brothers, had an irresistible urge for adventure. Throughout the mid-1930s Martin had become convinced that war in Europe was inevitable. News from the family relations in Germany of the alarming political developments there served to intensify this belief. The Herford family were not political, but they were very disturbed by the tales emerging in the press and recounted by their German cousins of the burgeoning concentration camps. Hitler's viciously anti-Semitic views had been quite clear since the publication of *Mein Kampf* in 1925, but even until 1945 the policy of mass destruction was hardly known about outside Germany. But inside Germany the signs were clearly marked long before the war broke out. Martin's cousin warned him that Hitler would be liquidating as many Jews as he could. Already fear of the Gestapo and SS had taken hold of the civilian population, and people would whisper fearfully to one another that they would 'go up the chimney' if accused of being subversives. The use of this expression was the first indication that ordinary German's knew something about the existence of gas chambers, and would later be cited as evidence that the people acquiesced in the formation of the concentration camp system.

Martin was determined to put his medical skills to good use and already had it in mind to become an army doctor. George joined the RAF, but had just qualified as a pilot at Montrose in 1936 when an untimely tragedy snatched away his life before war even started. On leave, two of his fellow officers egged him on to join them in hiring a sailing dinghy on the river Esk. George was reluctant as the weather was bitterly cold, and the river in flood and full of ice blocks. As well as this, only one man claimed to be an experienced sailor. It was a situation in which no sailing should have been allowed, but the three of them nevertheless set off for a trip out to sea. They quickly got into trouble as they hit a cross current where the river met the sea. As they attempted to turn back, the boat capsised, and only one of the young airmen survived – ironically, the man who had been most keen to go.

George's death had a profound effect on the entire family, especially Martin, who had become very close to his younger brother. Harold travelled back from India to attend the funeral. It was a time of immeasurable sadness. None of them could help feeling that the whole escapade had been a terrible and avoidable mistake.

CHAPTER 2

THE SPANISH CIVIL WAR

On 18 July 1936 the Spanish army began its rebellion against the Republican government. It was initially intended by General Franco and his rebel army officers to be a rapid seizure of key operational centres resulting in a successful coup within a few weeks. The reality was a bloody three year civil war. A third political force, the anarchists, took the military uprising as their cue to launch a social revolution to overthrow the State and replace it with libertarian communism. Within days fighting had broken out across the length and breadth of the country between Franco's military mutineers and the Republican army, and between Republicans and the anarchists, who were barricading the Barcelona streets. From the outset Italy and Germany lent military support to Franco's nationalists, and used the conflict as a dress rehearsal for the saturation bombing of civilian populations which was the scourge of the Second World War.

By November 1936 public opinion in Britain had been roused against Franco's Fascists, and a broad based campaign stretching across the political spectrum was organised to send medical and food aid to the beleaguered Spanish republicans, who were seen to be in the forefront of the struggle against European fascism. On 30 November the Albert Hall was the scene of a massed rally organised to support the teams of British doctors and nurses being dispatched to Spain. The aid was exclusively funded by public collections and charitable organisations. Dr Charles Brook, Secretary of the Spanish Medical Aid Committee, told the shocked Albert Hall audience that even the International and British Red Cross organisations had refused help because this was not a war between nations, and how the British voluntary unit already in Spain had been forced to paint over its red crosses because Franco's planes had made them a target, in total contravention of international law.

The effect of the Spanish Civil War on the British population has been largely ignored by historians. Even A J P Taylor wrote that the war 'remained very much a question for the few, an episode in English intellectual history . . . Most English people displayed little concern. They wanted peace.' This comment seems to have been made in almost total ignorance to the tens of thousands of ordinary people who organised marches, demonstrations, bazaars and appeals to raise more than £2 million for Spanish Aid (more than £65 million in current terms). Millions of people attended fund raising events. The result was the sending of more than 200 medical personnel with supplies, the setting up of many hospitals and ambulance services throughout Spain, the filling of 29 food ships from Britain and countless convoys of lorries filled by voluntary effort. Four thousand Basque children were brought by sea to Southampton and looked after in specially created homes, and more than two thousand British volunteers took part in the fight to preserve democracy.

Meanwhile, the British and French governments played no part and pursued a policy of non-intervention. This stance was adopted in order not to fan the flames of a potentially wider conflict on the continent. Even as the Spanish Civil War progressed and the involvement of Hitler and Mussolini deepened, it was still hoped that a broader war could be avoided. This was not a view shared by many of the working class organisations in Britain, who were actively engaged in the propaganda war against fascism from the early 1930s. For the international volunteers who took up arms against Franco, Spain was the only place in which fascism could be directly fought. Bob Selkirk, an unemployed miner who in 1936 was organising the National Unemployed Workers' Movement in Fifeshire, wrote, 'The

Fife workers supported the righteous struggle of the Spanish workers because they understood the truth embodied in the slogans, 'Bombs on Madrid mean bombs on London' – 'Fascism is the enemy of humanity.' These sentiments were certainly far ahead of contemporary government thinking. The official line was reported by *The Guardian's* diplomatic correspondent on 28 July 1936:

> 'There is every desire here to be on friendly terms with Spain, no matter what the complexion of the Spanish government might be. It is for these reasons – and one other – that strict neutrality is being observed. The other reason is that if some Powers, such as France or Great Britain, sells arms to one side, other Powers, such as Germany or Italy, may sell arms to the other. It is considered desirable that there shall be as few arms as possible in Spain and that there shall be no international complications.'

Among the first outsiders to bring Aid into Spain were the Quakers. On 25 December 1936 the first Quaker canteen had opened in Barcelona. Strictly speaking, Quakerism demands that absolute neutrality be observed, and that those to whom help is brought should be regarded merely as suffering people and not as partisans of a particular cause. However, in reality, their help was concentrated in Republican areas. Franco had taken care to occupy the main food producing regions, leaving two thirds of the population cut off from vital supplies.

Inspired by the Quaker's establishment of child 'colonies' in which displaced children were housed and fed and provided with medical treatment, and the canteens run in and around Barcelona, Martin, now Dr Herford, joined the relief effort soon after graduating by answering a newspaper advertisement calling for volunteers. In late January 1938, with the fighting still as vicious as ever, he travelled across France by train, and then by lorry into Barcelona.

The Catalan capital had witnessed some of the worst excesses of the war, and had been the victim of frequent air raids. The Republican government had moved its Headquarters north from Valencia to Barcelona in November 1937, leading the Republican population to fear that it had chosen this spot on the Mediterranean coast and close to the French border in preparation for a hasty evacuation. Franco responded with more air raids. Many were killed in a particularly heavy night attack on 3 January 1938. Three engined planes coming from the direction of Majorca dropped the bombs on the centre of the city. No military objectives were hit; Franco's aim was to terrorise and starve his opposition into capitulation. In the areas captured by his rebel forces he imposed a ruthless order and attempted to ensure the people were well fed, working on the assumption that a peaceful, normal and well-fed Spain was bound in the end to triumph over a revolutionary, abnormal and undernourished Spain.

Martin Herford arrived in Barcelona late at night in the cab of a lorry which crawled through the blackout with dimmed headlamps. The long wide streets were pitch-black, empty and deserted. He subsequently wrote in an article for *The Black Bag,* the journal of the Bristol medical faculty, that 'War is beastly, but civil war is particularly horrible. Where there is hate, there is always fear, and especially in civil war, there are individuals on both sides who wish to exterminate those they hate for fear that they may one day be strong.'

His work was concentrated in Barcelona and nearby towns. Throughout 1937 more than one million refugees had poured into north-eastern Spain. Many of the children had only summer clothes, and famine was imminent. Medical supplies, milk, soap and clothes came in sporadically, but shortages were acute. The refugees told stories of brutality, rape and murder committed by the Fascist troops, and especially the large Moorish contingent – behaviour in stark contrast to the standards of upright moral decency Franco claimed he stood for.

In December 1937 the American Friends Service Committee had made £200 a month available for relief in Catalonia. Herford arrived just as this money was being applied to the setting up of children's canteens in the Barcelona satellite towns of Sabadell and Manressa, and to creating more canteens in the city. By the end of the year there were more than fifteen such canteens in the area feeding five thousand children. The rations were minimal, just enough to maintain basic nourishment if they were lucky: the children were given a plate of porridge with milk and sugar each morning and a cup of cocoa each evening.

Other Quaker workers started a project to provide a midday meal in Barcelona's municipal schools. Kanty Cooper, a British sculptress who was in charge of this project, later wrote:

'I would drive a loaded van to a canteen with the certainty that the milk boxes, too heavy for the staff to lift, would be unloaded by unknown, underfed men passing in the street. We were working for the children they said, it was only right that they should help. No hand was ever stretched out for a tip.'

The other Quaker workers also found that although the local people were close to starvation, their lorries were not looted and their warehouses not broken into.

At the time, the concept of a large scale charitable relief effort was quite new to the British public. On his return to Britain Herford was plagued by curious enquiries as to what the relief workers ate when they were surrounded by the hunger – did they dine luxuriously or starve with the Spaniards. In fact they ate simply. Their diet consisted mainly of chick peas or lentils with a slice of bread, sometimes a little butter, some powdered milk and a little green salad. Occasionally they had a few biscuits of chocolate or tins of meat or fish. Anything less would have made the task impossible. The job involved hard physical labour, loading and unloading trucks, and in his first three months in Spain Herford recorded that he scarcely managed to get five hours sleep a night.

Outside Barcelona, providing aid for the constantly shifting rural population provided yet more challenges. The war fronts shifted rapidly, and when bombing began in one area tens of thousands of people would move quickly to another. On his return from England following a short period of leave, Herford was sent down the coast to Alicante to help set up a canteen for one thousand children. When he arrived the town contained eighty thousand people, and the air raids were becoming increasingly violent. He described the people there as nervous, 'with one ear cocked like rabbits – ready to bolt.' When the bombing intensified the town emptied, only about a thousand remained. The rest scattered across the countryside to forage for what little food they could find. It was better to be hungry and alive than fed and dead.

The people had every reason to be fearful, for the Fascists' proven policy was to wreak havoc on the civilian population, forcing most to flee, and killing those who remained. Possession of a trade union card, or mere suspicion of Republican sympathies could be enough to sign a death warrant. Whole villages would empty in advance of the rebel anticipation, with wagons piled high and dragged along ill-kept roads by over-burdened donkeys.

In Guernica in April 1937, Franco had shown that with the help of German bombers he was more than capable of wiping out large numbers of his countrymen at a stroke. Without warning, the German bombers swept over the Basque town no more than sixty feet above the ground dropping incendiary bombs. Anyone picking up the wounded in the street was shot down from above. An unnamed Basque woman gave her account to the Paris correspondent of *The Guardian*:

> 'Monday was market day, and the villagers of the neighbourhood were assembled at Guernica. At four o'clock in the afternoon, when the crowd was at its largest, an aeroplane appeared and dropped a few bombs, causing the first victims. The people fled from the marketplace to hide in the houses. New aeroplanes then appeared and bombarded the houses and churches. People were dying under the demolished ruins . . . they were obliged to run out, then they were fired on by machine guns . . . Many people remained lying in the street dead or wounded. In the houses you heard the wounded howling with pain. Many were burned alive under the ruins.
>
> When the house to which I had fled began to burn I ran like mad. Machine gun bullets continued to whistle round me, but I did not stop. When I got into a field I hid under a bush. People were running across the field trying to escape the bombs and bullets, which continued to pursue them. I remained under the bush until eight o'clock at night when it grew dark and the aeroplanes departed. Guernica by that time was nothing but a horrible bonfire.'

The levelling of Guernica was not an isolated incident perpetrated by over-zealous pilots. The magazine *Frankfurter Zeitung* reported a week before the raid that a new system of demoralising the unprotected 'Reds' had been devised which consisted of bombarding them first and then firing on them with machine guns. However, the Fascists immediately denied their involvement. The day after the bombardment of Guernica Reuters in London received a communiqué from the rebel G.H.Q. at Salamanca which read:

> 'The destruction of the richer part of Guernica . . . by the
> retreating Reds has aroused much indignation among our
> troops and is spurring them on to save the Basque people
> from the Communists who are destroying their property.'

To the intense frustration of Herford and his fellow relief workers, the country as a whole did not appear to be short of food, but it was concentrated in areas which were often impossible to get at. Good roads were few, and in the hilly country, thin and winding, and often impassable by large lorries. Valencia was the main source of outside supply for Republican Spain, situated conveniently on the eastern coast, but it was also the main supply route for Madrid, and food had to be driven 250 miles over a perilous road which in many places was badly damaged.

In the countryside, farming was carried out as it had been for many centuries. Even the steepest hill sides were terraced and planted with olives and vegetables. Almost all the work was done by hand, and Herford recalls seeing only two mechanical harvesters in the whole of his time in Spain, one of which was broken! In the areas in which the population remained sufficiently stable to produce a healthy crop, problems occurred with food hoarding. In Lerida the peasants amassed large stocks of wine, olive oil and wheat. When in April 1938 the town was routed by the rebels, they destroyed everything rather than let it fall into enemy hands. Only 100 miles away in Barcelona there was famine.

Although Herford's main role in Spain was organising the distribution of food to children, he had the opportunity on several occasions to visit hospitals caring for the Republicans. His strongest impression was of the Spaniard's capacity to endure great suffering. In a civilian hospital he visited in Madrid, there were five operating tables in a row in a single theatre and only five surgeons. Patients lay watching others being operated upon whilst waiting their turn. In another Madrid hospital he witnessed several thoracoplasty operations being carried out under scanty local anaesthetic; the procedure involved the removal of several ribs to facilitate the collapse of a diseased or injured lung!

Even this sight was not as tormenting as the wards in which those victims of the pellagra epidemic were lying, surrounded by swarms of black flies which infested the hospitals where supplies of disinfectants were short. The disease was caused by a deficiency of nicotinic acid (one of the B vitamins) in the diet, and is characterised by scaling of the skin, inflammation of the mouth, diarrhoea and finally dementia. Adequate supplies of milk could have prevented many thousands of painful deaths.

It was in Madrid that Herford got his first taste of being under heavy shell fire. The Republicans daily showered shells into some part of the city. Often they concentrated on the poorer districts, hoping to break public morale. But the people adapted remarkably quickly. It amazed Herford and his colleagues that life continued virtually as normal, the streets bustling with people going about their business. When a shell was heard everyone stood still. If it fell far away business continued, if it fell near they bolted for cover into basements and underground stations.

As aerial bombardment increased in the early months of 1938 – Franco's 'Blitzkreig' – it became increasingly clear that despite the defiant statements of their leaders, the Republicans were unable to resist the rebels' superior firepower. Herford noted that although Barcelona, to which he returned from Madrid, was badly bombed, it could easily have been destroyed. But Franco deliberately held off from flattening cities he expected to enter as a conqueror. Instead it was small towns and villages which bore the brunt. Herford visited the small town of Nules shortly after it was bombarded. Although it had been largely evacuated before the raid, hardly a single building had escaped damage. The Republican government issued a plea to Great Britain to drop its non-intervention policy and allow them to buy arms, but still it fell on deaf ears. Franco continued to blame his worst atrocities on the retreating 'Reds', and on the occasion of Germany's entry into Austria in March 1938, he sent a comradely telegram to Hitler:

'From the victorious front of the war against Communism I send your excellency the greetings of Spain and my own in this solemn hour in which Germany has rendered a service to the West by sparing Europe danger and bloodshed.'

In Barcelona the small amount of resistance that could be offered from anti-aircraft guns was wholly unsuccessful. In forty consecutive air raids, not one plane was shot down. Herford watched on many occasions as the bombers flew serenely on through puffs of white smoke from exploding shells. Even at night the raids continued. The Republicans swept the air with searchlight and tracer fire, but to little effect. German and Italian pilots were sent over in increasingly large numbers, rehearsing for the bigger conflict which was still to come. Towards the end of March 1938 the Republicans mustered their first chaser planes, and the crowds in the street cheered enthusiastically as they took to the skies. But as Herford recorded at the time, 'they never seemed to get into the air in time.' Defeat was becoming inevitable.

Herford had a narrow escape himself, when he and Arthur Walker were standing on the roof of a six-storey building looking out across the city and suddenly bombs began to fall. The explosions got nearer and nearer, until a missile exploded almost on top of them. The whole building swayed with the force of the blast, feeling for a moment as if it was about to topple. Fortunately it remained upright, but was partially destroyed.

In April 1938 Franco's forces cut Republican Spain in half when they broke through to the sea at Vinaroz. The only way to travel between Barcelona and Valencia was by air. Shortly after this occurred, Malcolm de Lillihook, the Commissioner of the Sweden-based International Commission for Child Relief, came to Barcelona to collate information for a report on the food shortages throughout Spain. Herford had the good fortune to be invited to accompany him on a three week whistle-stop tour of the country. Edith Pye, the head of the Quaker relief effort, had persuaded a number of outside organisations to form a joint Commission which would collect funds from foreign governments with the aim of providing a hot meal each day for every Spanish child in need. For the most part the Quakers were going to be responsible for administering the funds on the ground.

Before leaving Barcelona Herford accompanied Malcolm de Lillihook on a visit to no lesser person than the head of the Republican government, Prime Minister Dr Juan Negrin, and his Foreign Minister, Alvarez del Vayo. Negrin was a thickset, dark and quiet man with a kindly face. Before the war he had been a Professor of Medicine at Barcelona university. Malcolm de Lillihook explained that as they represented a humanitarian non-partisan organisation, it was planned to help children on both sides of the conflict. In marked contrast to the callousness of Franco, Negrin replied, 'I sincerely hope you will, for they are all Spanish children. I shall be most grateful for anything you can do to spare them suffering.' Dr Negrin then saw to it that they were issued with special passes which required civil and military authorities to facilitate their journey at any time.

When Herford set off by air from Barcelona to Valencia it was his first flight. It was a memorable experience. They took off before dawn and swept outwards into the Mediterranean over a sea of white cloud lit by a full moon; then descended at dawn to see a patchwork of orchards, cornfields, vineyards and red-tiled, white-walled houses in the fertile land near the coast. From the air the countryside looked almost sublimely peaceful.

In a military hospital near Valencia Herford met another prominent Republican, Largo Caballero, Negrin's predecessor, who had resigned in May 1937. Ideologically, Caballero was a radical socialist. One of Franco's generals said of him, 'It is only mistaken ideas about sanitation and hygiene which have allowed rats like him to live. It is wrong to encourage scum to breed.' Herford asked him why all Republican Hospitals had a bust of President Azana on display.

Caballero replied with more than a hint of irreverence that 'General Miaja wished it'. Miaja was the greatest of the Republican Generals, one of those who had remained loyal to the Republic after the rebellion began. Caballero's attitude was symptomatic of the divisions within Republican ranks. As Herford observed, men fought for many different and individual reasons, some for the independence of their particular homelands, the Basque region, Catalonia or Valencia, others for a wider socialist revolution. The Republican side was a broad alliance of many different interests, whose downfall was due in no small part to their internal differences.

On returning to Valencia to take an Air France flight back to Barcelona, Herford and de Lillihook were caught in a particularly heavy air raid. As they were driven into town to get the signature of the police official who had to authorise their travel, the whine of the falling bombs grew louder, and the clouds of dust and smoke thrown up by the exploding shells closer. They made it to what they thought was the correct government office, only to find that due to air raids it had been moved. The streets were virtually deserted and there were very few passers-by from whom to ask directions. They drove through the air raid from one building to the next, until finally Herford managed to find the official who had to sign their papers. But their troubles were not over. The car was running low on fuel and wouldn't make it to the air strip. They tore through the city searching for an operational petrol pump.

By the time they had refuelled the air raid was over and crowds of people were emerging from their hiding places and filling up the roads and pavements. The car was slowed to a snail's pace. In desperation the driver stepped on the pedal horn, even though he had strict orders to use it only in an emergency. Two girls in the street called out, 'Los syronos!' and people began to scatter. Never having used the horn before, the driver mistook it for the real thing and panicked, he promptly stopped the car and ran for cover.

Twenty minutes later he emerged from the shelter to be berated by his angry passengers. They raced through the rubble strewn streets in time to see the plane roar into the air.

Fortunately they did not remain stranded for long. By a stroke of good fortune they heard that the British cruiser *Arethusa*, the flag ship of the Mediterranean, was about to collect a few refugees and some British journalists from the nearby town of Gandic. They made it to the dock just in time and were given magnificent hospitality by the Captain. Malcolm de Lillihook had the Admiral's cabin and Herford the Captain's. Herford has remarked that he has never been graced with such VIP treatment since.

Immediately after leaving port the Captain received an order over the radio to examine the British oil tanker SS *Union*, which had suffered a direct hit and was on fire outside Valencia harbour. They drew alongside the burning tanker, but the surviving crew had already disembarked and escaped to land. Nearby, the passengers and sailors on deck could see the mast tops of seven other ships which in the preceding month had all been sunk by Franco's bombers. Among them was a cargo ship which had been loaded with 6,500 tons of grain. It had received a direct hit and had sunk in under ten minutes.

It was carrying enough food for tens of thousands of people – far more than any single relief organisation could have brought in.

In July 1938 Herford returned to England to report, to help raise money and get some deserved rest. The work had been hard, and relief workers had to be strong and fresh to be of any use. But during his leave events in Spain accelerated. Fighting had intensified near Barcelona and it was considered unwise by the Society of Friends to risk the lives of any more relief workers than was necessary. In October 1938 the British volunteers in the International Brigade were sent home by the Republican government who ordered the withdrawal of all non-Spanish combatants. In January 1939 Franco captured Barcelona, and in March, Madrid. On the night of 29 March Mussolini addressed a ten thousand strong crowd and told them:

> 'Franco's infantry and the Italian legionaries have entered Madrid, and the Spanish war can thus be considered finished. It finished with the collapse of Bolshevism. So will end all enemies of Italy and of Fascism.'

Hitler also welcomed the news, and sent a telegram to Franco congratulating him on 'the final defeat of nation destroying Bolshevism'.

Herford was bitterly disappointed at not being able to stay in Spain until the end, but also realised that since qualifying he had made no practical use of his medical training and had not held a hospital post. His experiences in Spain reinforced his conviction that war with Germany was only months away. Until he had taken a hospital job he would not be able to practice, so in September 1938 he accepted an appointment in Cossham Memorial hospital near Bristol and gained his first practical experience in surgery. In March 1939 he moved to Bristol General Hospital where, when war was declared, he was already a house surgeon in the ear, nose and throat department. He immediately tried to enlist in the RAF, but in the

41

expectation of heavy air raid casualties hospital doctors were classified as belonging to a reserved profession and were forbidden from joining any of the Services. For several frustrating months it looked as if he would be confined to the home front for the duration.

CHAPTER 3

The Finnish Expedition

By February 1940 Herford's patience was running out. He made a special plea to the RAF to be allowed to join on the grounds that he wanted to belong to the same service as his brother George, but the reply was slow in coming. Whilst the bureaucratic wheels were turning, he chanced upon an advertisement in *The Times* appealing for volunteers to join the newly formed Finnish Aid Bureau (FAB). The Bureau was an independent organisation, quite separate from the regular services which was privately funded by several very wealthy philanthropists. Its independence meant that those who were otherwise prevented from joining the services could be enlisted by the Bureau.

Finland had been invaded by the Russians in November 1939, and the FAB was frantically recruiting volunteers to join the British Contingent of an International Volunteer Brigade. Whilst there was much popular support for the Finns in their struggle against the Soviets, it was considered extremely unlikely that the British government would declare war on Russia as well as Germany. Assuming that the war with Germany would shortly spread to Scandinavia, Herford decided that his only chance of seeing military action was to offer himself as a volunteer. He wrote immediately to the Bureau's offices in London, and the next day received a telegram asking him to come at once.

Russia's war with Finland was less an ideological than a logistic one. Stalin wished to secure a longer coastline on the Gulf of Finland for the protection of Leningrad, and to push the Russian border back to claim Karelia, the north eastern region of Finland. Twenty-six

Soviet divisions comprising 465,000 men, were pitted against a slender Finnish army of 130,000. The Russians were so confident of a swift victory that many of the soldiers were only equipped with summer uniforms. However, after an horrific air raid in Helsinki on the first day of the war, the Finns put up dogged resistance and held up the invasion force in a series of bloody battles.

The Russians were superior in numbers, but the Finns' intimate knowledge of the terrain and their ability to cope with the extreme temperatures gave them the edge. The columns of Soviet tanks and troops often had to move single file along narrow forest roads in freezing conditions. The Finns manoeuvred quickly on skis and bicycles and adopted highly successful guerrilla tactics. Using crude but effective methods, they roamed around like packs of wolves and ambushed tanks with petrol bombs thrown into the turrets (the 'Molotov cocktail', first used in Spain against Franco's German and Italian tanks). Tank traps were dug to disable the lead vehicle in a column, and the caterpillar tracks from the drive wheels were prised away with logs. By these methods the Russians would be brought to halt in the desolate pine forests. If they stayed in their vehicles any length of time they froze to death. If they left their tanks they foundered in the soft snow; if they lit fires to keep themselves alive they became targets for Finnish snipers lurking in the woods. The Finnish newspapers carried photographs of long lines of snow-covered Russian transport and tanks next to which were huddled heaps of Russian soldiers, frozen to death or shot.

Herford reported to the hectic and disorganised London offices of the FAB where he was asked if he would lead an ambulance unit consisting of four ambulances, a travelling dispensary and staff to deal with air raid casualties and to help initiate typhus control. He was at once struck by the atmosphere of confusion which seemed to characterise the whole ad-hoc operation. These initial fears proved to be well founded.

A week later Herford reported back to the FAB medical advisor, Lord Dawson of Penn, for an examination. He was also asked a few brief questions about his training and experience. After only cursory questioning he was told that he seemed suitable for the job. Herford enquired about the rate of pay for volunteers, and was pleasantly surprised to hear that they would receive the equivalent pay to personnel in the RAMC (Royal Army Medical Corps). Had he read the small print in the contract which was hastily presented to him, he would have realised that whilst in Finland, he would only be paid the equivalent to a Finnish officer of similar rank, the balance being paid into a London bank account. In the event, nothing found its way into the English account. This was only one of many disillusionments which were to follow with the entire expedition.

Maladministration in the FAB was evident from day one. Initially Herford was told that he would not be required to travel for three weeks as the ambulances were not yet ready, but three days later he received a telegram requiring him to come to London the next day ready to depart. He telephoned the Headquarters and was told by a subordinate to disregard the wire. There was such an air of doubt about the message that Herford telephoned several times until he was able to speak to the man in charge, Mr Gibson. Gibson was amazed that he had been told to disregard the telegram, and asked him to be in London the following afternoon.

Herford arrived in London early the next morning and went immediately to Lillywhites to be fitted out with battledress, some tough ski boots and cold weather clothing for Finland. Acquiring the correct clothing was the responsibility of the volunteers, who were to travel in civilian clothing and change into uniform and assume rank on arrival. That morning Lillywhites was bursting with the strange variety of men who were making up the expeditionary force.

Overwhelmed assistants were pulling all kinds of garment off the racks, and the men were kiting themselves out in clothing with little consideration to the extreme ferocity of the Finnish winter.

In the rush Herford had found time to arrange a last minute farewell lunch with his sister Sylvia, and Mary, a fellow student from Bristol. He had no idea how long he would be gone, but was thinking in terms of months rather than years. In fact, he would not be returning to England for nearly four years. Sylvia was a practising doctor at the Royal Free Hospital, and Mary was working in the Bristol Royal Infirmary. (While many of the consultants were away during the war, she became an extremely well respected Acting Senior Registrar, and organised the evacuation to Newcastle.)

Mary was studying medicine at Bristol. Whilst still students she and Martin had struck up a friendship which in time became a courtship, in the conventional sense of the word. Even in war, relationships continued to proceed in a formal fashion. They had never discussed the future of their relationship, as everything was so uncertain, but there seemed to be an implicit understanding between them that their unspoken mutual affection would in due course become an engagement. Herford was not a great romantic. Had he been, this would have been the perfect opportunity for him to confess his love for her and to propose, before leaving to face an uncertain fate. Instead, he treated Mary no differently from his sister; he bought them both lunch and presented them with identical presents – a pair of gloves.

Was this lack of outward passion a mark of insensitivity, or the complete reverse? Herford knew one thing: that he could offer no long term guarantees, and that any attempt to make plans for the future would be marred with uncertainty. He was not a man to make promises he couldn't keep. But there was more between them than either let on to the other, and that afternoon they parted in no doubt that they were committed to one another. Having said his goodbyes,

46

Herford joined the other volunteers at a drill hall near King's Cross station where they were gathering before taking the night train to Leith. In an attempt to instil a little military smartness they were called to attention and briefly addressed by Colonel Rooseveldt, whom they were told would be shortly be following them out to Finland and taking charge. This information was greeted with some scepticism, as when Rooseveldt stepped forward he was visibly suffering from uncontrollable tremors, and looked most unwell, creating the distinct impression that he was quite unfit to lead them.

The sense of foreboding was intensified when Gibson called Herford aside and asked him to take control of £500 in mixed sterling and Scandinavian currencies, which was to be used to cover emergency expenses en route; on arrival in Finland the remaining money was to be handed over to the paymaster, who was already in situ with an advance party. Herford accepted this responsibility reluctantly, but was offered little choice. The large bundles of notes were stuffed into his suitcase without being counted, a signature was scribbled on a receipt, and he was driven hastily through the gloom of the blackout to the station feeling like one of a band of conspirators on a wild clandestine mission.

At the station Herford was introduced to Captain Blew-Jones (ex-Life Guards), a six foot four giant of a man who was to command the draft; Fraser, his diminutive assistant; and Major Joyce, a thin man in his sixties who had come out of retirement from the army to be second in command. The volunteers were divided into platoons of thirty, each with two men in charge who were to assume the status of officer and senior NCO on arrival. Like most of the FABs' arrangements, these were also made incompetently, as many more volunteers had been promised officer status than positions were available, providing the fuel for many acrimonious disputes and petty power struggles.

47

The Finnish volunteers left British soil in a large convoy on 9 March 1940. The sea voyage aboard the SS *Meteor* (rumoured to be the ex-Kaiser's yacht) took four days. Herford busied himself securing the use of the ship's dispensary and taking stock of their extremely limited medical supplies. Most of the others divided themselves up into little groups and spent the time playing cards and generating rumours about each other's pasts. They were an incongruous mixture of men with very little in common with one another apart from being on board the same ship. Rather like French Legionnaires, many of them had enlisted to escape, some from drinking and gambling debts, others from situations which they didn't care to discuss. Strangest of all were the wealthy young men who had never been anything but West-End playboys. Only a handful seemed to be there because of their convictions. Finding himself amongst this raggle-taggle collection of individuals, Herford was already becoming concerned for the future of their expedition. He had quickly had cause to become deeply suspicious of Blew-Jones, who was not acting like a responsible commanding officer. For most of the voyage he was holed up in his cabin with Fraser working his way through a crate of whiskey, and after several days he summoned Herford and demanded that he hand over the £500. Herford at first resisted, but when Blew-Jones made it an order he had no choice but to capitulate. He could see no reason why it was necessary for Blew-Jones to have control of the money unless he was harbouring a dishonest motive.

Unknown to the outside world, peace talks were taking place between the Finnish Prime Minister, Risto Ryti, and the Russians in Moscow even though the war in Finland was still raging. Since early February the Finnish army had been in retreat, ground down by sheer force of numbers. On 10 February the Russians attacked the Mannerheim line north east of Helsinki with such ferocity that they broke through the Finnish defences. The Finns fell back to a second line half a mile to the rear, but three days later the Russians broke through again. These successes were owed to a massive squandering of Russian lives by their commanders. Using the 'crescendo offensive,' a phrase coined by Marshal Voroshilov, the Soviet Minister of Defence, wave after wave of troops were sent in one after another until the exhausted enemy were finally beaten down. This primitive strategy claimed the lives of 27,000 Finnish soldiers and 58,000 Russians.

On 11 March impassioned pleas were still being broadcast on the radio for more Finnish volunteers, but the next day an armistice was announced. The war had come to an end the day before the volunteers arrived. The defeated Finland was forced to cede large areas of the Baltic coast to the Russians as well as granting them a thirty-year lease of the strategically important Hango Peninsular on the southernmost tip of the country. This settlement gave the Russians a dominant position on both sides of the Gulf of Finland.

The following morning the *Meteor* docked in the Norwegian port of Bergen. Blew-Jones and his ever-present assistant, Fraser, went ahead of the others to seek instructions from the British consul. They returned with the answer that they were to proceed as planned to Lapua in Finland, the central point for all volunteer contingents. The peace was still considered fragile, and it was felt that British troops might soon be needed to counteract the anticipated German invasion of Norway.

The motley unit was sent across Norway and Sweden by night train and the following day arrived in Happaranda, a small town just inside the Swedish border, where the temperature was between minus 20 and 30 degrees. The men were then herded into a large barn-like building where General Sir Ormonde L'Eppee Winter KBE CMG DSO, the representative of the Finnish Aid Bureau, and an ageing veteran of the previous war, was to have met them. It turned out that he had bronchitis and was too ill to come, which only reinforced the overall sense of anti-climax.

After the parade, Blew-Jones and Fraser sneaked off for a private interview with the General, and returned with the news that apart from Blew-Jones and Joyce, who was to hold the rank of Major (he had commanded the first Heavy Machine Gun unit in the First World War and won an MC), no others were to be considered as officers by the Finns and that Herford would therefore have to rank as an ordinary volunteer. Herford was indignant, and reminded them that he had been specifically told that he would assume the rank of Lieutenant on his arrival, and would refuse to be treated as anything other than an officer. Such was the disorganisation that Blew-Jones was in no position to gainsay him, but the antagonism between them was already evident. Blew-Jones and Fraser were clearly mounting a systematic attempt to wrest control of the entire expedition, but Herford was determined to be a thorn in their flesh.

The volunteers finally arrived in Lapua on 25 March. The men were billeted in primitive, cramped barracks in a large hall, and Herford and Major Joyce were put up in a local farm. Blew-Jones and Fraser had chosen separate lodgings in another comfortable farmhouse by themselves. Also stationed in the town were a detachment of Finnish soldiers and an advance party of forty British volunteers under the command of Captain Chandler and his 2nd Lieutenant, Guthrie.

Blew-Jones' manoeuvrings took a new twist when, shortly after their arrival, Chandler and Guthrie invited a party of officers, including several Finns, to their quarters for tea. They had received a telegram which was causing them some concern. Herford and Joyce were excluded from the discussion, but finally Joyce took the telegram and read it: it was from 'D'Hiver H.Q. British Troops' and purported to appoint Blew-Jones a full Colonel. On the way back to the billets Joyce was deeply puzzled by the instruction, until finally he turned to Herford and announced that it must have been a fraud, sent by Fraser during their journey to Lapua.

By the time Herford returned to Chandler's quarters the following day the telegram had indeed been exposed as a fraud and Blew-Jones and Fraser ordered to leave the unit and return to Sweden. Herford insisted that a proper investigation first take place into their handling of the unit's funds, so Fraser was asked to produce an account. In the event he came up with a spurious and inept document which failed even to disguise his clumsy dishonesty. All the money which Herford had handed over to Blew-Jones had been converted by him into Finnish marks at an exchange rate very favourable to himself. When asked to give a personal explanation he was tongue tied, and several packets of money were found in his coat pockets. In total, he had misappropriated over £100 of the FAB's money. To Herford's amazement, however, no punitive action was taken; and, after producing the missing money, Fraser and Blew-Jones were simply dispatched to Sweden.

The following day General Enkell of the Finnish army announced that all volunteers were free to return to Britain immediately via Sweden. Those who wished to remain, in the event they could be of no service, would be returned at a later date. About seventy returned but got no further than Sweden. Herford opted to remain in the hope that a use would be found for him, and threw himself into combat training.

It was late March, and temperatures were still falling as low as minus 40 degrees, but the volunteers were brought into a semblance of order and taught drill, marksmanship and skiing. Herford made best use of his limited medical supplies, but had little other than minor ailments and dysentery to deal with. His main problems continued to be with the other officers. Having rid himself of Blew-Jones, Chandler sought to secure his position by threatening Herford with summary dismissal when he complained at the way in which the contingent was being run. Chandler had now elevated his own assistant, Guthrie, to the position of second in command while completely ignoring the superior talents of many others, including Major Joyce, who, unlike Guthrie, had served as a regular soldier.

The situation was further aggravated in mid-April when the German army invaded Denmark and Norway. The British responded with their own landing in Norway, and the Finnish volunteers were anxious to join them. Battle was raging between the Allied troops and the German forces, and severe casualties were inflicted by the German air force. Finally permission was granted for those who wanted to, to go to the northern Finnish town of Rovaniemi and from there to Narvik in Norway to join the British expeditionary force. But, whilst they were waiting to be moved from Rovaniemi the Norwegians capitulated and the British withdrew. The volunteers were sent back to Lapua without having come within 100 miles of action. Morale sunk to its lowest point yet.

By the end of April, the initial attractiveness of Finland with its picturesque snow-laden forests, had worn thin. The winter was reputed to have been the coldest for a century and the food was insufficient and monotonous. The few lighter moments that occurred were scarcely enough to raise their spirits out of the doldrums.

Some of those who made the best of being marooned were a party of three hundred Hungarian volunteers. Their language, like that of the Estonians, was similar to Finnish. They were great singers, especially on the march, and some of their songs made the worst the British could offer seem tame. Among them was an enormous Padre, well over six feet in his socks, who had a particularly fine baritone voice, an admirable capacity for alcohol, and an ungodly appetite for women.

He had taken part in guerrilla fighting on the Czechoslovak border and at one stage had been caught by enemy troops who proceeded to hang him by the neck from a tree. Fortunately his executioners were disturbed by the return of his own party, who cut him down and managed to revive him with artificial respiration.

In mid-May the British contingent were finally moved from Lapua to the far more attractive town of Savonlinna. Spring had finally arrived, and when the men were not training they were able to swim in the clear lakes and sunbathe on the shore, a far cry from the desperate struggle that was at the same time taking place in and around Dunkirk.

This contented atmosphere was given an extra fillip by the arrival of a group of FANYS – British women volunteer nurses, who accompanied the men on canoe trips and an excursion on a pleasure steamer. But unfortunately the women did not stay long, and left Petsamo in a ship bound for America. En route they were intercepted by a British cruiser and had the good fortune to be taken straight back to England. Had it been a German cruiser, the British passengers would certainly have been arrested. By a further stroke of luck, in November the OC of the FANYS, Miss Runciman, found herself at a dinner in Newcastle with Herford's 'fiancée', Mary, and was able to show her a number of suitably innocent photographs of him and the other volunteers taken in Finland. It was the first news Mary had had of Martin's existence since his departure as none of the volunteers' letters had arrived home.

In the middle of June the volunteers were visited by Lord Balfour, President of the Scottish National Provincial Bank and a senior figure in the FAB. In an ill-considered speech he promised that strenuous efforts were being made to get them returned to England. In fact, two ships had been chartered for the purpose, but one was sunk and the other diverted to carry out more urgent tasks. All available craft were being thrown into the war effort, and a potentially dangerous ferrying operation across the North Sea was not considered a high priority. Herford and two fellow officers took the opportunity during Balfour's visit to complain vigorously about the inadequacies of Chandler, their Commanding Officer, and his assistant, Guthrie, whom he had recently promoted to full lieutenant. Herford also expressed his frustration with the entire situation – as far as he was concerned the FAB was not only grossly inefficient, it was also acting highly irresponsibly by keeping the volunteers from active service.

Balfour appeared to listen carefully and promised to take the matters up with the British legation in Helsinki. The result was a visit two weeks later from another official, Colonel Gill, the British Military Attaché in Finland. Colonel Gill appealed for patience, and promised a ship would be arriving shortly. But his promises amounted to no more than a cynical attempt at appeasement.

The only positive effect of these two visits was the removal of Chandler and Guthrie and their replacement with Lieutenant Ruck-Keene. The promised ship of course did not materialise, and the volunteers were moved on again to the town of Jyvaskyla. At this stage the military nature of the expedition ceased. A telegram was received from London stating that all volunteers would revert to the rank of private and were to be encouraged where possible to earn their own living. Pay was to be cut to that of a private's, except for those who succeeded in finding work, who would not be paid at all. Volunteers reverted to civilian dress and all training ceased.

The weeks spent in Jyvaskyla were far from hard when compared with what the rest of the war would bring. Herford made friends of some local families and learned a little of the impossibly difficult Finnish language. He played tennis and football with some of the workers from the local plywood factory, skied on the remaining snow and took frequent saunas followed by plunges in the lake. He also made the surprising discovery that many of the Finns had strongly pro-German sentiments, and expected Finland to declare war on the Russians on the side of Germany. The general feeling was that the war would be over in six weeks and that Russia would have to return all it had stolen from Finland. Some extremists even talked of acquiring Leningrad, but they were few in number. These views were held in obvious ignorance of the more despicable aspects of the Nazi regime, but may go some way to explain the reason why a sterner attitude was not taken towards Germany by the European democracies throughout the 1930s. It was the spectre of communism and Soviet imperialism which was most widely feared. A strong Germany was considered a useful buffer against potential Soviet aggression.

Week after week of inactivity was more than Herford and many of the other volunteers could stand, and they started to formulate plans for making their own way out of the country. Herford's first escape attempt was in September. He made enquiries among the men and was finally put in touch with one member of a party of Finns who was planning to leave the country imminently, and would be prepared to part with his identification papers for the right price. Suspecting his contact of being unreliable, Herford arranged to meet him in Helsinki, planning to pay him at the last possible moment before departure, thereby minimising the risk of being turned in and the man claiming his papers back from the police!

For the plan to work successfully a reliable companion was needed, and Herford was lucky enough to secure the help of a fellow volunteer, Aiken-Quark. A 'veteran' pilot from the Spanish civil war who had gone on to earn a handsome living in currency exchange and smuggling from Algeciras and Gibraltar, he was an adventurer to whom the planned escape was a piece of welcome excitement. They decided that the two of them would board the train with the party bound for Petsamo, and that the transfer of papers would take place during the journey. Half the money would be handed over during the journey, and the other half would be retained by Aiken-Qaurk who would leave the train with the seller at a halt before Petsamo and pay him the balance when Herford was safely out of the country.

Everything went to plan in Helsinki, and Herford and Aiken-

Quark managed to by-pass the Finnish police who were making a very careful check of the passengers' documents. The problem came from an unexpected source. One of the passengers on the train was a Dutchman who had been a volunteer and who recognised Herford. Guessing that he did not have the proper papers, he made an official protest to the Finnish police. He and Aiken-Quark were ordered from the train at the next halt. Fortunately the seller had not yet been paid! They managed to put up in a small railway inn and returned to Helsinki by the morning train.

It was the beginning of November before another escape opportunity arose. The British contingent had now been moved to Korpilahti, and as there were very few medical duties to perform, Herford was able to take up the invitation of Professor Holsti, Dean of the Medical School in Helsinki, to stay with his family and tour the capital's medical facilities and clinics. During this trip he heard a rumour that some volunteers who had got into Sweden earlier in the year had managed to get transit visas for Russia, Turkey and Palestine, where they joined up with British forces in the Middle East. It was a chink of light, but the problem was getting into Sweden.

Until this time, all applications to the British Legation in Helsinki for Swedish visas had been refused, even to the son of a former British ambassador to Stockholm. However, Herford made enquiries of the British Embassy in Stockholm and found that the Councillor there had been at the Barcelona Embassy in 1938 and had been particularly sympathetic to the Quaker relief effort. He wrote back saying that he could not interfere with legation in Helsinki, but enclosed a letter from Sir Archie Ross, the son of an old friend of Herford's father whom he had not seen for many years, and who was now third Secretary in Stockholm. He offered to help in any way he could.

The Finnish passport office required two referees in Sweden. Herford used the names of Malcolm de Lillihook (with whom he had kept in contact), and Sir Archie Ross. When Ross's name was mentioned, the official exclaimed, 'Do you know him? He's a very good friend of the official in charge of the passport department of the Swedish Foreign Office. If you mention his name you are sure to get a visa.'

A week later his Swedish visa arrived. The next step was obtaining a Russian transit visa. Another back door opened when Herford secured an interview with the Finnish Minister of Finance, Herr Vinoe Tanner, through a former volunteer who was now tutor to Tanner's children. Although Tanner was a personal friend of Madame Kollontai, the Russian Ambassador in Stockholm, he thought in view of the current tense relations between Russia and Finland, the best course was to give Herford an introduction to the Swedish Prime Minister, Gustav Müller.

That it took such high level assistance simply to secure a visa, was symptomatic of the wartime bureaucracy. Without the right friends Herford might have been trapped in Finland for the rest of the war.

CHAPTER 4

Stockholm to Cairo

In early December 1940, as the first snows were falling, Herford set off by train to the port of D'Abo, from where he crossed the Gulf of Bothnia to Stockholm. Having been so long in Finland, with its food shortages and barely stocked shops, he had forgotten what it was like to be faced with a choice of anything. The first thing that struck him about Stockholm was the sumptuousness of it all. The city exuded wealth and opulence. The shops were overflowing with almost everything one could desire – fine clothes, beautifully crafted furniture, fresh fruit wrapped in shiny coloured paper and mountains of exquisitely made pastries and cakes, their coloured icing twinkling like jewels in the shop windows. The existence of such luxuries had almost entirely vanished from his memory. In contrast to the dimly lit shops and thoroughfares of Helsinki, Stockholm was ablaze with light and colour. It was as if the war had scarcely touched this neutral country and its supply lines remained open to the four corners of the world.

Herford made straight for the restaurants and feasted first his eyes, then his stomach on forgotten delicacies and some that were altogether new. The only warm drink on offer in Finland was tea consisting of a few sorry leaves scattered into hot water. One of the first things he tried in Sweden was coffee with thick, rich cream and sugar. He went to the Openkeller, a famous restaurant which specialised in *smorgasbord* and he sat down to a table spread with forty small dishes, each one different, and enjoyed a sumptuous feast. Herford has remarked that after the extremely limited fare of Finland, he came to Sweden with an eye which rested rather ravenously on food.

Herford's first port of call on business was the offices of Malcolm de Lillihook. The two men had got on well together in Spain and de Lillihook was charming and affable, and more than willing to help. He immediately arranged for Herford to present his letter of introduction to Herr Müller, the Prime Minister.

Herford met with Herr Müller shortly afterwards. He was a tall, heavily built man, with typically Scandinavian features. His bearing was confident and he had a manner which gave the impression of considerable force of character. Müller asked keenly after his friend Tanner, and then enquired about Herford's plans. He listened patiently while Herford described the Finland debacle and his plan to travel across Russia, showing a level of genuine interest in a relatively trivial matter, which was quite extraordinary, given his position. Müller then wrote a letter of introduction to the Soviet Minister.

Continuing his tour of the influential people of Stockholm, Herford visited Archie Ross, who used his influence to secure a meeting with Madame Kollontai, the Soviet Ambassador.

It was with some trepidation that he mounted the steps to the Soviet Embassy. Madame Kollontai was a larger than life figure from a former world, who had somehow successfully survived the transition to Bolshevism. She had been born into an aristocratic family and was considered a great beauty. Before the revolution she had married and become well known in the wealthy, French speaking upper classes in Leningrad. But as unrest grew she became active in progressive and revolutionary circles and had written a book on free love – *Freedom of Women* – which had been widely read. She became a close personal friend of Lenin and soon after the revolution was appointed Commissar of Public Welfare, and later moved to her Stockholm post, a position which she held until 1943. When she was finally relieved of her post, she continued to live in Sweden until her death. This was almost exceptional, as in the Stalinist era many Soviet Ambassadors held their posts for less than a year and were recalled to Russia never to be heard of again.

Herford was received in the hallway of the Soviet legation by one of the secretaries, who took his details and led him into Madame Kollontai's room. After a few minutes she swept through the door in a most regal fashion, a slight, erect figure dressed in a plain black gown, her only ornament a gold locket hanging from a simple gold chain. She had a high forehead and slender, refined features which still bore the traces of her youthful beauty. Her secretary bowed in a most courtly manner, showing not the merest hint of communist equality. Herford had been pre-warned that the Ambassador expected her callers to kiss her hand in the manner of the old regime, and she daily extended it in the manner of a queen greeting a subject. Herford reacted by shaking her hand in the conventional way. If she felt put out by this error she disguised it very tactfully.

Their conversation was short and carried out mostly in French, as she spoke little English and Herford no Russian. She asked a few formal questions and said that she would send to Moscow to ask permission for a transit visa.

It normally took several weeks for visas to be processed and Herford's Swedish visa lasted only for a week. But through another stroke of luck, he was introduced to the Director of Medical Services in Sweden by Malcolm de Lillihook, who was related to the official in charge of the passport office. A three week extension of his Swedish visa was 'arranged'. But after only five days the Russian visa came through, and with much regret Herford had to cancel plans to tour the Stockholm hospitals with the Director. Instead he was forced to return to the relative gloom of Helsinki and spend Christmas with the remnants of the volunteers waiting for the British Embassy to secure the Turkish, Syrian and Palestinian passports he needed to finish his journey.

Before leaving Finland Herford managed to stir up a hornet's nest when he wrote letters to several senior figures in the FAB setting out his catalogue of criticisms of the entire handling of the Finnish expedition, and enclosing verbatim transcripts of the speeches made by Lord Balfour and Colonel Gill promising the volunteers a speedy return. He was firmly of the view that this had been nothing more than hot air, and even deliberate misinformation. Knowing that they could not be expected to arrive in England for many months he requested of the British Embassy that they be carried to England in diplomatic bags. Three days later he was invited to an interview with Gordon Verreker, the British Ambassador, who was very troubled by the letters' contents, and insisted that they were amended before they were carried. He also reminded Herford that he should consider his long term career, and also that of Colonel Gill's. But Herford would not back down, and with a few alterations the letters were apparently sent in a diplomatic bag. Unfortunately they never reached their ultimate destination!

It was 4 January 1941 before the formalities were finally completed and Herford boarded the Leningrad train in Helsinki station. The British Embassy had advised him not to travel with any binoculars, camera or papers, and in a fit of defiant disgust he tore up a very detailed diary of events he had compiled since being in Finland – an act which later became a source of deep regret.

The light faded early, and the train proceeded along the coast in darkness past the twinkling lights of Vipuri, a Finnish port which had been ceded to the Russians at the conclusion of the war. Just outside the town the train drew up and all passengers were transferred to a waiting Russian train. As Herford crossed the platform he saw his first Russians – soldiers tramping up and down in thick sheepskin coats and heavy boots, bracing themselves against the freezing night.

Compared to the Finnish train carriages, the Russian ones were comfortably warm, and the customs officials, far from being ogres, were neatly dressed and treated the passengers politely. Herford communicated as best he could with sign language, and produced his papers and opened his luggage for inspection. Against the Embassy's advice he had brought camera, field glasses and a number of photographs, but none of these seemed to attract their interest. They made a cursory search of his possessions and then examined every square inch of the carriage, including the straps on the cushions. They were either concerned about hidden bombs or were operating on the assumption that any intelligent smuggler or enemy agent would take care to hide any incriminating evidence carefully and somewhere where he could disassociate himself from it. Herford was understandably pleased that as the only Englishman aboard the train he had not been the object of their scrutiny.

The train rumbled into Leningrad station at 1 a.m. Waiting on the platform was the representative of Intourist, the official travel agency. All foreign visitors had either to be on an organised Intourist tour, or accompanied by an official guide. The man spoke English and was cheerful and courteous, insisting that Herford should not carry his own bags. He called over two of the burly station porters and led the way to a taxi.

The taxi sped through the deserted streets, over the Neva Bridge and past the Hermitage to a large hotel opposite St Isaac's Cathedral. The hotel, like most of central Leningrad, was of grandiose nineteenth century proportions. The main lobby was ornamented with faded guilt fittings, and the aged furniture was upholstered in red velvet. A display cabinet contained a collection of shoddy over-priced china and fancy goods. The whole effect was of decayed opulence, as if for the last twenty-five years time had stood still.

The guide was busily arranging breakfast and a taxi to the station in the morning when Herford told him he had not booked a room, as it cost £4 and he was only to be there a few hours. The guide apologised profusely, and said that in that case he would have to pay for the taxis, porters and breakfast. It would cost around 80 roubles. Herford carried out a quick mental calculation – he had a letter of credit for £100, an English £10 note and a few dollars. The Russians were notorious for ruthlessly extracting foreign currency at very unfavourable rates of exchange, and the few dollars he had would fall far short of what he needed to pay his bills in Leningrad and Odessa, his next port of call. The receptionist offered to cash a letter of credit or traveller's cheque for roubles, but there would be no way of changing roubles back into hard currency.

Remembering a story he had been told by an acquaintance in Helsinki, he asked the receptionist if there were any second hand goods or pawn shops in the area. 'Of course not!' she replied, astonished at the question, and added, 'You wouldn't expect to find such places in London or Paris.' Herford assured her that both cities were full of them, but she clearly did not believe him, and reacted as if he had uttered a vile slur against her country.

The story had been told to him by an accountant from the British firm Price Waterhouse in Helsinki, and concerned a colleague who had been flying to Cairo from Stockholm via Moscow. But when he arrived in Moscow he was told that there would be no onward train for a week. He had been expecting a non-stop journey and had very little money with him. All he could do was to go to the British Embassy and ask advice. To his surprise one of the officials asked him if he had a spare suit he would be willing to part with. Intrigued, he replied that he had. The official asked him to bring it along the next morning. When he arrived the following day with his suit, the official handed him 5,000 roubles, and the accountant spent the rest of the week dining on champagne and caviar.

Wondering if he could pull off a similar feat, Herford dozed fitfully in an armchair until 6 a.m., when he took a swift breakfast, then slipped unnoticed from the hotel. As he needed only a few hundred roubles, he ventured out into the snowy streets with his best woollen scarf and several pairs of socks hoping to find a customer. Even at this time in the morning, the still-dark streets were filling with people, and queues were beginning to form outside shops, and even next to some very meagre handcarts standing by the kerb. Herford went into one of the shops and saw that it was moderately well stocked with groceries; German sausages, cheese and vegetables. Each item was individually priced, and probably far too expensive for the average citizen. Using sign language, he pointed to the cheese trying to communicate that he wished to buy some, but the shop keeper seemed to be asking him to produce a card of some sort. Evidently there was a system of rationing in operation, and Herford left empty handed.

By the time daylight arrived his wandering led him to what appeared to be one of the main shopping areas of the city. The buildings were tall and elegant, and the shop fronts impressive and ornate, but on close examination there was little behind the facades, and no window displays. The few goods for sale were scanty and cheap. The only exceptions were a few much smaller shops which seemed to be trading in second hand clothes.

Time was passing quickly, and Herford had to make some rapid progress if he was to raise enough money to pay the hotel expenses. He cast his eye along the passers-by. They were heavily wrapped in sheepskins or thick woollen overcoats and their heads covered with the traditional fur hats, the only headgear capable of keeping out the biting chill. In cold weather, the Russians have a way of walking purposefully along, their eyes glued to ground in front of them and their faces set in a sullen frown. It was with some difficulty that Herford tried to pick out some who looked as if they might be able to

64

answer him in French or German. He began by innocently asking the way, but had little luck, not appreciating that even if he was being understood, it was simply not safe for a Russian to be seen speaking to a foreigner, and especially not about black-marketeering, or 'speculation' (the derisory term applied to all forms of capitalist activity).

After drawing several blanks, a frail old lady finally stopped and replied in excellent French. She was happy to chat for a minute or two, and said that she had been in London many years ago for a short time, and had a sister there who was a teacher of languages. Herford eventually asked her if she knew anyone who would be interested in buying a suit. Her eyes lit up. 'Is it as good as that one?' she asked, and took off her glove to feel the material, stroking it reverently. He assured her it was. She said that she had a friend who would be interested and asked where he had the suit. He arranged for her to come to his hotel in a short while, and she scurried off to find her friend.

Only after parting did it occur to him that the friend would probably be very reluctant to come to an official hotel to transact illegal business. He couldn't afford to entrust the situation to chance, so he decided to try his luck in the second hand shops. Naturally the shop keepers were very suspicious of the foreigner, and refused to buy, perhaps suspecting a trick by the secret police. But one of the proprietors did speak a little German, however, and gave Herford an address where he said he might be more successful.

He tried a third shop and was again unsuccessful. As he was coming out he was accosted by a small, scruffy man who spoke some very slangy German. He had seen him attempt to sell the scarf and socks and said he could help him find a buyer. Herford followed him into another clothes shop where a huddle of people had accumulated. The man spoke to the manager and nodded in Herford's direction, but the manager shook his head. Fear of trickery by the secret police was so ingrained that the risk was simply too great to take. But the conversation had been overheard by a number of customers, who followed him out onto the pavement. Herford suddenly found himself surrounded by eager faces. A hefty sailor forced his way to the front and asked how much he wanted. Herford asked the scruffy little man – who was now firmly established as his interpreter – how much he should charge. He replied, 500 roubles for the scarf and 300 for the socks. Herford told the sailor he could have the scarf and a pair of socks for 300. The sailor handed over the money and with no attempt to bargain went away very happy.

As the small crowd disappeared back into the shop, the interpreter became disgruntled that Herford had sold for so little. Herford replied that should any questions be asked, it would reflect better on him if he sold at a low price; that way he could not be accused of cynical exploitation. Besides which, he still had several pairs of socks to sell, and decided to visit the address the shop manager had given him. He tipped the Russian 50 roubles and got some detailed directions from him. There was no argument over this small gratuity, the man took the money and left.

The walk to the address took about ten minutes, and Herford found himself entering a scruffier residential area. He showed the scribbled address to a passer-by who pointed to an enormous eighteenth century tenement surrounding a large stone courtyard. He walked up three flights of flagstone steps and into a rundown desolate hallway off which were the numbered front doors to the flats.

He knocked on one of the doors, which was opened by a poorly dressed, unwashed woman who looked distinctively apprehensive. He showed her the address, and she pointed across the hallway to another apartment and quickly closed her door. He crossed the hall and knocked again. After a considerable interval he heard some slow shuffling steps and another dishevelled woman in a threadbare dress answered and peered out at him from the gloom beyond. He strained to see into the darkened interior, but could make nothing out. The air was heavy, and gave the impression of dirt and staleness. The woman stared at him with suspicious eyes. Herford felt uneasy, he didn't like the look of the place and beat a hasty retreat. As he turned, he saw the door across the hallway was slightly ajar, and the first woman was staring out at him. As soon as their eyes met she slammed it shut. Visitors were evidently not welcome.

Safe in the knowledge that he now had enough money to pay his way, and had an hour or two before the taxi would take him to the station, Herford wandered along the streets observing the people and buildings. Western visitors were a rarity, and he seized the chance to drink in his surroundings. Behind the impressive facades the general poverty was self evident. There was little traffic, much of it horse drawn with a few ancient looking cars. The bulk of the population had always endured hardship and for the most part were pacified by what Stalin told them – that in the West poverty was far worse, and that capitalism was starving the workers to death.

Herford's eye was caught by a watch-repairers in a graceful premises that looked as if it had once been a fashionable jewellers. Now its display cases were dusty and bare. The only items in the window were a few old clocks that could have come out of an East End jumble sale. As he carried on along the pavement he must have glanced at his wrist watch, for a man suddenly appeared at his side and in a garbled mix of Russian and German tried to offer several thousand roubles for it. He was very disappointed when Herford refused, and tramped away crestfallen.

One of the chief contrasts with western cities was the complete absence of advertising hoardings, except for large propaganda posters proclaiming the glory of the government and the achievements of Soviet soldiers and workers. There were also many posters which seemed to be encouraging people to learn to ski – perhaps in response to the severe losses sustained in the Finnish war. Parties of school children and naval cadets marched past carrying skis over their shoulders. They looked surprisingly fit and well fed considering the lack of supplies in the shops.

The Odessa train left at midday, so Herford returned to the hotel at 10.30, the time at which he had arranged to meet the prospective customer for his suit. As he had expected, no one arrived. When he went to the desk to pay his bill, the receptionist failed to conceal her surprise at his producing roubles instead of dollars.

The guide returned to escort him to the station, presuming that his charge had not left the confines of the hotel. Fortunately the outing had passed without attracting any interest from the army of secret police which infested the city.

The station was a heavy mass of drab humanity, whose unwashed smell immediately assaulted the delicate British nose. They had apparently been waiting to board a train which had not yet left the station. They clung resolutely to every spare inch of the carriages, but could not possibly have hoped to survive the cold once the train got under way! Herford was greatly relieved to find that they were not trying to board the Odessa train.

There were two classes of travel on Russian trains; hard and soft. Hard meant unreserved wooden benches and a bumpy ride. Herford was booked into the soft class, and had a sleeping bunk in the carriages reserved for officials. Many of the other passengers appeared to be army officers, and in contrast to the chaos in the rest of the station the platform was clear and orderly. Each carriage was presided over by a railway guide who showed the passenger to their compartment. There were four berths in each, but the bunk above Herford's had a broken strap, and so he had a whole side to himself.

He said goodbye to his guide who hurried away without taking a tip. The train groaned ominously then pulled off with a violent jerk. Passengers soon learned to brace themselves against this attempted fracture of the couplings which occurred after every stop.

The berth was neat and comfortable. There was a thick feather mattress, an eiderdown and pillow, all in clean white covers. Herford's two travelling companions for the next forty-eight hours were a frail woman in her seventies and a younger man who was evidently her son. She was clearly not in good health. Their clothes were clean and tidy, but almost threadbare, and their luggage was squeezed into a rickety old hamper and a large washing basket. The man's more valuable personal possessions were tied up in a red bandanna handkerchief of the kind workmen used to carry their sandwiches. But despite their outward appearance of poverty, they seemed very kindly and refined people.

When the train was underway Herford broke the ice by getting out his primus stove and brewing up some tea, and was pleased to discover that the man spoke enough German for them to carry on a halting conversation. At first they merely exchanged pleasantries and small talk, and as they headed south the man pointed out one of the former palaces of the Czars which stands not far from Leningrad, a magnificent colonnaded building which rose imposingly out of the bare winter landscape.

The first day passed without the Russian and his mother engaging in anything other than cautious polite conversation, over cups of tea brewed on the primus, and when the man spoke, Herford noticed that it was in hushed tones and only when the compartment door was closed. The man did not tell Herford his name, but was not so reticent when it came to expressing an interest in his tinned provisions and his supply of bread, butter and cheese, all of which were apparently in very short supply in Russia, and which he was only too happy to share.

During the brief hours of daylight Herford spent much time watching the landscape race by, and noticed many Russian soldiers in the fields learning the skills of cross-country skiing. Later that year, when the Germans invaded Russia, the Russians employed ski-borne troops and made ingenious use of machine guns and anti-tank guns mounted on sleighs, some of them powered and driven by aeroplane propellers. The Germans would find themselves at the same disadvantage as the Russians ambushed in the Finnish forests.

On the second day Herford woke early and was washed and shaved before most of the other passengers had stirred. He shared another cup of tea with his companions, and much to his pleasure found that he had begun to win their trust. He gleaned that the man was an engineer who specialised in mining problems. He did not discuss the details of his work, but was obviously a technical expert who had been of considerable use to the government and who had now reached a highly responsible position. He said that his duties took him all over Russia – from Vladivostock to Moscow, to Odessa and to Baku on the Caspian Sea. Herford told them of his adventures in Leningrad, and to his surprise the man asked if he still wanted to sell the suit. Herford said he could spare it, and sold it for the bargain price of 600 roubles.

The subject which fascinated the Russians most was the comparative conditions in their two countries. The man said candidly that the position across the whole country was bad; essential supplies were short and millions lived in extreme poverty. Moscow was the main commercial centre and was comparatively wealthy. However, Leningrad came a long way behind, next Odessa, and after that conditions deteriorated yet further. In the smaller towns and villages which housed most of the population, the peasants lived no differently from their grandfathers, without basic services such as electricity and sanitation. They endured conditions far inferior to those of the labourers and workers of Western Europe, and if they fell ill, the chances of receiving proper medical treatment were slender. Rural doctors tended to be extremely ignorant, and in some areas medical qualifications could practically be bought.

Even for the middle classes, existence was hand to mouth. The average salary was between 8,000 and 10,000 roubles per month, which was barely sufficient to cover essentials – when they were available. As soon as a shop received a supply of a desirable item such as pairs of boots, word would spread through the neighbourhood and a queue soon formed. People would wait in hope for hours, only to be turned away empty handed. Simple items such as Herford's pencils were considered a rare luxury. It was almost impossible, he said, to get any good pencils in Russia, but they were essential tools for a draughtsman. A few years previously he had succeeded in getting a supply from abroad and had been the subject of great envy among his colleagues.

The Russian diet was very simple. The main staple was black bread. Very little fat or meat was available, but they had a certain amount of dried fish and a limited variety of vegetables, mostly potatoes. There were only two classes of person who could acquire more than the basic necessities: the producers, who could use their produce to barter for other goods, and the party executives, who often received 'luxury goods' in lieu of salary. Those who rose to senior positions in the party could live the life of a millionaire. The upper hierarchy had cars, expensive clothes, exotic foods, houses and even palaces by the Black Sea, but money couldn't buy them, only favour.

Herford asked whether the army had also fallen victim to the shortages, and whether this would compromise their ability to fight. The Russian replied that much of the deprivation was due to so much being spent on equipping the army for what was viewed as an almost inevitable war with Germany. But on the question of whether the army would be able to stave off any German invasion he had definite and confident opinions. Any army that attempted to invade Russia, he said, would suffer the same fate as Napoleon's. They would be swallowed up by distance and inadequate communications, and the winter would be an overwhelming enemy. In Russia the distances were too great to establish a Maginot line, but instead their armies were organised to create strong points, and all their defences and supplies were at the ready. Leningrad might fall, and even Moscow, but they were prepared to fight back to the Urals and beyond. 'We can buy time with distance and no line of communication will be safe; they will be too long,' he said.

By the end of the second day the two had formed a friendship, but knew they were unlikely ever to see each other again. The Russian said goodbye whilst still in the train, saying that it would be safer if when in Odessa they appeared not to know one another. They shook hands warmly and parted. Moments later they passed on the station platform like complete strangers and went their separate ways.

Herford was to spend the rest of the day and the night in Odessa before sailing the next morning for Turkey. It was the major port of the Ukraine, a beautiful, geometrically set out city built high on the cliff tops overlooking the Black Sea. In the summer it was a coastal resort, and the area around the city was renowned for its beautiful gardens and vineyards. But in January the cold was as cruel as it had been in Leningrad.

This time his Intourist guide was an attractive young girl of about twenty-five, who took him on a taxi tour of the town and arranged for him to see the ballet 'Esmerelda'. Herford lost no time in asking her if she could arrange for him to visit the city's hospital. His request was again met with astonishment, 'You wouldn't like it if foreign doctors insisted on intruding into your hospitals in England,' she responded. Herford explained that on the contrary, he would be delighted. He felt strongly that doctors were an international community whose duties transcended all forms of political dogma. The guide eventually agreed to seek permission, but was flatly refused!

The following day Herford boarded the SS *Srenatia* at dusk. Again he experienced no difficulties with the border guards, who, having ascertained that he was a British doctor, waved him through without searching his luggage.

The night was cold and clear, and the sheets of loose ice on the water glinted in the bright moonlight. The glittering lights of the town lit up the harbour in an almost magical way. It was a calm, unsuspecting city, one of the most attractive of old Russia, which due to the loyalty and resolve of its people retained its dignity despite the harshness of the communist regime. But Odessa and much of western Russia would shortly be going the way of eastern Europe. Later in the year the Germans came first with bombs and then with an invasion force which claimed the lives of hundreds of thousands of Russian troops and civilians. On 22 October 1941 Odessa was the scene of one of the worst massacres of Jews seen in Russia. At noon the previous day Hitler said of the Jews, 'By exterminating this pest, we shall do humanity a service of which our soldiers can have no idea.' 25,000 Jews were rounded up in the city, half of whom were locked into four vast warehouses, three of which were set on fire. Those who sought to escape death in the flames by escaping through the holes in the roof or windows were murdered with a hail of bullets and machine gun fire. Many women went mad, throwing their children out of the windows. The fourth warehouse was then destroyed by artillery. But for now, Odessa was basking in its last precious moments of peace.

The two day voyage was punctuated by a brief stop in Varna, the main Black Sea Port of Bulgaria, but passengers were not allowed ashore. Bulgaria was vacillating in her loyalties and was hostile to all foreigners. Weeks later, on 1 March, King Boris of Bulgaria acquiesced to the Germans and signed his country's allegiance to the Berlin-Rome Axis, providing Germany with a much needed pathway to northern Greece.

Shortly after noon on the second day of the journey, Herford had his first view of the shores of neutral Turkey. As they neared land, a steep, rocky coastline bore up out of the azure sea, behind which were green fields, reminding him of parts of Cornwall. The winter sun was shining brightly, and reflected off the roofs of the higgledy-piggledy whitewashed houses of the little fishing villages and the flotillas of brightly painted fishing boats cluttering every inlet. From the deck Herford had his first view of a middle eastern landscape, the olive groves on the hillsides, the trellised vines in the villages and the high wooden frames on the quays on which the fishermen hung their nets. After the grim northern climate it was an uplifting and tantalising sight.

The ship docked in the bustling port of Constantinople and Herford took a taxi through the crowded streets to the British Consulate. The Consul was a friendly, efficient man who said that he had been given instructions to send all volunteers arriving in Turkey through Egypt on third class tickets. This instruction had mystified him, as in Turkey only the lowest peasant and labourers travelled third class. He had therefore taken it upon himself to issue second class tickets, and arranged for Herford to take the train the following day and suggested a pleasant hotel in which to stay, and a selection of local restaurants which would give him authentic Turkish cuisine.

The Hotel Pera stood at the summit of one of the city's hills, and commanded views of both the old and the new towns. Much of the old quarter had not been changed since the Middle Ages, a low lying maze of labyrinthine streets connected by pungent narrow alleyways which occasionally led into little courtyards, quiet oases amidst the clamour of the traffic and street traders.

Although the Turkish travel visa debarred halts, Herford decided not to take the early train for Ankara the following day, but to spend his limited time taking in the sights of the city. He strolled down the hill into the narrow, cobbled streets, and was surprised by the number of soldiers he saw, short mahogany faced men with rough features, dressed in crumpled khaki tunics with soft boots and long criss-crossing puttees worn up to the knees. He was watching the passers-by and admiring the outside of one of the many ornate gold-topped mosques when he was approached by a pleasant but insistent Turk who produced a handful of visiting cards from English tourists and said he was an experienced guide. Herford preferred to be independent, but the guide was quite insistent. When Herford finally made him understand that he really didn't want his services, he said that he had nothing to do for the next hour or two, so he might as well spend the time with someone who could help him improve his English. Herford had little choice in the matter.

The guide led the way on a whistle-stop tour of the city. They went into the Blue Mosque and viewed the enormous dome, and into the military museum which was filled with ancient weapons and memorabilia. Herford then asked the guide if they could see inside the nearby military hospital. To his great surprise the request was granted, and a young army doctor showed them around the wards and operating theatres. The facilities were simple, but well equipped and efficiently run and probably far superior to those in Russia. The highlight of the day was the bazaar. Set in what was reputed to be the stables of ancient Constantinople, dating form 400 BC, the bazaar was a tangled network of dark, low buildings housing a myriad of tiny shops hidden behind secretive little doorways. The vendors sat in these darkened interiors sipping small cups of thick black coffee and smoking sweet Turkish cigarettes. The air was filled with rich aromas, some of them perfumed and exotic, others far less pleasant.

A native lunch of figs, oranges and Turkish Delight was followed by an encounter with several souvenir shops where Herford was initiated into the art of bartering for pretty trinkets for Mary and relatives at home. For a man who favoured straight talking, haggling didn't come easily, and he found the quick witted traders running rings around him, weaving an enticing web of words until they ensnared their unwitting prey. He emerged from the bazaar wiser and poorer.

As a token of thanks Herford offered his guide the equivalent of about 15/-, but the man refused this sum with a look of indignation, and produced from his pocket a letter setting out the official pay scale which he said entitled him to at least 30/-. Herford protested that he had forced his services onto the unwary traveller, insisting that he had nothing better to do. The guide became more and more irate. Rather than provoke an unseemly scene – which would not have been long in coming – Herford parted with more than £1, and the guide trounced off with the air of one unjustly used.

The train to Ankara thundered along the coast next to the sea of Marmara through olive groves and small fertile patches of land cultivated with fruit and vegetables, before rising into arid mountainous country in which the track wound across perilous viaducts and along thin cuttings carved out of the jagged hillsides. The landscape here was barren and rocky, an inhospitable place that would only sustain the hardiest sheep and goats and the wiry peasants who eked out a fragile existence amongst the rock and scrub.

The train arrived in Ankara early the following morning. The city itself was modern, and set on a high plateau which had once been malarious swamp land. Much of the scrub had been drained to make way for building, but the outlying areas were still swamp and water. Herford was to stay one night. He reported to the British Embassy who checked him into a hotel and gave him another £6 to cover his travelling expenses. He made a small tour of the town, but it was not as attractive as Constantinople and the travelling was taking its toll. He made for his bed and slept soundly.

The Taurus Express bound for Beirut passed through equally dramatic hill country, snaking through high desolate gorges scorched by the sun in summer and in the winter buried deep in snow. Herford was within a day of his final destination and the welcome borders of the British Empire.

As the railway descended towards the frontier it passed through what was then the longest tunnel in the world, blasted out of solid rock, before arriving in the pleasant greenery of the Syrian low country, in stark contrast to the barren Turkish uplands. After a brief overnight stop in the border town of Aleppo, the train pushed on to Beirut.

Herford again had only time for the briefest reconnoitre of the beautiful coastal city, which at that time might have been the south of France. He walked through the old town past shady cafes and dark little shops and along a dusty road into the countryside beyond, passing native French speaking troops dressed in long, flowing uniforms. The soothing quiet of the olive groves was a tremendous relief after the clatter of the city and the claustrophobia of the train. It was mid-winter, but the sun shone brilliantly off the bright yellow sand and white-walled houses. Of all the places he had passed through, Beirut was the most appealing. He could have spent a lot longer, enjoying its fine French colonial architecture and civilised ambience, but first thing the following morning the train left for Palestine.

When he first caught sight of the Union Jack fluttering over the frontier post Herford felt an unexpected thrill at being back on 'home territory'. Here the border controls were tight, and Herford made the mistake of being foolishly honest. When asked how much currency he had in his possession he admitted his several pound notes and a single £10 note, which he had changed at the request of the military attaché in Finland some months previously. He was instructed that £10 could be taken into the country and that the rest would be sent on for collection in Cairo. Herford kept the £10 note, but the official neglected to tell him that it would be impossible to change. From the border post the train took them on the final leg of the journey to Haifa, where Herford promptly reported to the Movement Control Officer(MCO), who arranged for his onward journey to Cairo the next day.

When it came to settling the hotel bill the following morning the £10 note was flatly rejected. The bank and the police also refused to change it. The bank made close enquiries as to where the money had come from. Herford then learned that he had in fact been planted with what was for all intents and purposes dud money. The bank regretted his tale of woe but said they were unable to help. £10 notes were far too large a denomination to be in frequent circulation, besides which, there were widespread fears of counterfeit currency being introduced by the enemy in an effort to sabotage the economy. Thankfully Herford's almost uncanny good luck held, and another hotel guest saved the day when he negotiated with the frontier police to get Herford's other currency back – he was a senior customs official!

As Herford later observed, the whole journey went like clockwork. There were minor hitches, but fate always leant a hand and ensured him a smooth passage. An operation which had been organised with military precision could not have run more smoothly. Although he didn't realise it at the time, he had a guardian angel who wouldn't leave his side for the next four years.

Apart from more painfully detailed questioning about the origin of the £10 note at the Egyptian border, and a meticulously close examination of all his personal papers, the final leg of the long haul to Cairo passed without incident. Although, had Herford run into the military attaché who planted the note on him, he would probably not have stopped at verbal retaliation.

The next morning was 19 January 1941. Herford had lost all count of time and had forgotten it was a Sunday. When he arrived at the British Embassy there was only a junior ADC on duty. But the ADC put him in touch with Squadron Leader Sinclair, his personal contact in the RAF, who in turn referred him to Air Commodore Panter, the Principal RAF Medical Officer.

Until now, Herford had not thought of joining any service other than the RAF, but when Commodore·Panter outlined the duties of a station MO, he was sorely disappointed. He realised that the job would be both administrative and a long way from the scene of action. But medical officers were in short supply in the RAF, and as far as Panter was concerned, Herford had been granted his passage from Finland on the understanding that he was enlisting on arrival. He was therefore surprised and more than a little put out when he announced that he would like to have an interview with the Royal Army Medical Corps before finally committing himself.

Colonel MacFie and Colonel Hacker of the RAMC were equally hungry for new recruits. Far from being tucked away behind friendly lines, the MO, RAMC, would be highly mobile, travelling in a field ambulance and supervising the collection of casualties from the battlefield. The conditions under which the MOs and their orderlies worked were as perilous as those endured by the troops. The red crosses painted on the ambulances and tin hats would hopefully offer some protection against enemy gunfire, but the medical staff were virtually unarmed and in a highly vulnerable position. Herford was impressed with this brief and decided there was no comparison between the challenge of the RAMC and the relatively pedestrian duties he would be stuck with in the RAF.

Two days after his initial interview Herford received his

commission as a Lieutenant with the RAMC. There was only one minor difficulty – apart from a letter of introduction from the British Ambassador in Helsinki referring to him as a doctor, he had no other proof of his qualifications. All his personal correspondence, which might have provided a little additional evidence of his bona fides, was with the censors. But with a touching faith in his veracity, the army took his word as sufficient, and he was posted for duty at 63 General Hospital at Helmieh.

CHAPTER 5

The Expedition to Greece

To Herford's initial disappointment, the 63 General Hospital was not busy when he took up his post on 22 January 1941, and he found that his medical duties were far from arduous. There was little military action taking place, so there were few casualties to be dealt with. Herford felt frustrated – he hadn't travelled all the way to Egypt to treat dysentery and minor illnesses. But luckily the hospital was near to the great pyramids, and he lost no time in sightseeing and climbing to their summits.

If he had possessed a little more patience he would soon have been caught up in the battles in the Western Desert, but he was itching to be of use in the front line of wherever he could. When he heard that preparations were being made for an expedition to Greece, and that Lt Colonel Mollan, the Officer Commanding the Hospital Medical Division had been posted to take the command of 24 Casualty Clearing Station, he instantly volunteered himself and pleaded with Mollan to have him on his staff. Unable to resist this impetuosity, Mollan agreed, and on 27 February Herford was attached to his unit.

When Herford reported to Alexandria docks along with three fellow officers, Fulton, Robertson and Elmazor on 7 March, he had been in the army all of five weeks, and had barely learned how to wear the uniform correctly, but he was being sent as part of the British expeditionary force which aimed to bolster the Greeks against attack from the Germans who were rapidly progressing through Yugoslavia and Bulgaria to the northern borders of Greece. The southernmost European state, with its enormous coastline and prime strategic position was a possession greatly desired by Hitler. The expeditionary force of 100,000 men was mounted following the advice of Anthony Eden, the then British Foreign Secretary. The objective of the British War Cabinet was to establish a 'Balkan Front' across Greece and Yugoslavia. This would both arrest Germany's southwards march, and provide bases from which British bombers could attack the Romanian oil refineries which were Germany's principal sources of oil.

Herford describes his state of mind as he set off as a ship's medical officer as 'guileless and optimistic'. His thoughts were still far removed from the grizzly realities of war, and far from being consumed with nervous anticipation at what he might find in the coming weeks, he admired the clear blue waters of the Mediterranean and soaked up the warm sun on the deck of the sturdy cargo vessel, *The Settler*, which carried them across to Piraeus.

Although the British population and armed forces were still in good spirits, even despite the massive air raid casualties which had already claimed tens of thousand of victims in the major cities, the early months of 1941 were arguably the nadir of the war for the Allied forces. Whilst sailing to Greece, Herford had a conversation with a young officer of the 4th Hussars who asked him, 'Do you know the difference between the expedition to France and ours to Greece?'

'No', Herford replied.

'The difference is,' the young officer explained with a grim smile, 'that no one expected Dunkirk and so the evacuation was successful, whereas everybody expects an evacuation of Greece, so it will inevitably be a disaster.'

Herford recalls that this brief exchange opened his eyes for the first time to the possibility of becoming embroiled in the full ugliness of war. Thus far thoughts of his own mortality and the prospect of failure had barely impinged on his unfailingly sanguine outlook. Now it occurred to him that perhaps he had made a mistake in bringing along his tennis racquet and gear. Unfortunately the young officer's comment was alarmingly astute. The Allied forces would quickly be driven from Greece with heavy losses. Historians have unanimously concluded that at the very least, the Greek expedition was an overly optimistic enterprise which served only to waste valuable military resources.

With his heart now beating a little faster in his chest, on the dawn of 11 March Herford pondered portentous events as the convoy in which *The Settler* was travelling drew into Piraeus harbour. There was a thick mist hanging over the water and a bite in the crisp early morning air. As the troops disembarked there was a tangible sense of foreboding. There was something disconcertingly amateurish about the whole enterprise. Greece was counting the minutes until the fighting began. She was a country under a deadly threat.

Herford's initial destination was the 25th General Hospital in Kifisia, about 10 miles from Athens. The Greek countryside through which they passed was verdant with spring. In stark contrast to the Egyptian desert, the Grecian earth was deep red and the hills and fields were bursting with green shoots, canopied vines, fruit trees and spring corn. The outward appearance was of a quiet and peaceful country populated by relatively poor but contented farmers.

The hospital at Kifisia was situated near the Pendelicon quarries, from whence the stone was hewn which was used to build the Parthenon. Behind the town were mountains, the highest of which was Mount Pendelicon, which soon after their arrival was adorned with a mantle of snow. Not overburdened with work, as there were not yet any casualties, Herford and two fellow officers, Major Harvey and Major Pugh, set out to climb the mountain behind the hospital. Harvey had been in Greece some time at the 26th General Hospital, and had the distinction of having cared for the former Greek President, Metaxis, in his final illness. Major Pugh was an enthusiastic skier and mountaineer, and was extremely interested in the physiological effects of strenuous exercise at high altitudes. The mountain slopes were far colder than the mild valleys below, but the snow was melting in the waxing winter sun and yielding to the shoots of tiny irises, snowdrops, crocuses and other wild flowers which carpeted the hills in swathes of stunning colour throughout the spring. At the summit the air was brilliantly clear; on one side of the mountain was a panoramic view over the Gulf of Boetia to Marathon, on the other the bay of Salamis. The hills either side were shielded from the late afternoon sun and looked bleak and cold, black and rocky, streaked with snow and patches of scrub. The upland country was wild and gloriously untamed. Herford was more at home looking out at the world from a windy mountain top than anywhere else. He opened every pore and tried to soak it in.

Several days later the unit was moved by train to a camp ten miles west of Larissa, a substantial town situated 150 miles north east of Athens, and some 30 miles from the Aegean shore at which roads intersect from all the major towns of the north east, making it a position of major importance. There was still little sense of urgency, and the fine spring weather succeeded in easing away the anxieties which had built up in the days immediately after landing.

The unit erected camp in a valley and awaited the arrival of the bulk of their equipment. In this unhurried climate they could again drink in the beauty of their pastoral surroundings. In the distance to the north was the impressive snow-covered peak of Mount Olympus. In the foreground were rolling downs, covered in shooting corn. Large flocks of sheep grazed quietly under the watchful eyes of weather-grizzled shepherds with huge and fearsome dogs. The first week spent here was light-hearted and peaceful – a far cry from the events which were to follow.

Herford learned a valuable lesson in campcraft, as applicable to the boyscout as to the battle-hardened soldier, when, a few days after striking camp, the heavens opened and a mighty storm shook the

84

valley with cracks of thunder that seemed to make the ground itself shake. Mount Olympus disappeared into a swirl of racing black clouds. One could instantly comprehend how earlier civilisations came to fear the wrath of the Gods who dwelt on its summit. As the tents had been pitched on a hillside, they were in danger of simply being washed away in the deluge. Before the full force of the storm hit, Herford grabbed an entrenching tool and furiously dug a trench around his tent, finishing just as the full blast made itself felt. He dived inside for cover, not knowing whether his bed would shortly be swept down the mountain in the fast moving sheet of water which was already pouring down the slopes. Fortunately his quick work paid off. The trench was filled almost to bursting, but the tent remained dry.

The following day a warning was issued to expect German parachutists. A week earlier Bulgaria had given in to the Germans, as had Yugoslavia. However, the Yugoslav government and the Prince Regent, Prince Paul, were overthrown by an almost spontaneous revolution and the heir to the throne, the seventeen year old King Peter, was installed as Head of State. The new government of General Simovic withdrew from the pact with Germany and Italy, incurring Hitler's wrath. On 26 March six hundred aircraft were flown to Romanian and Bulgarian airfields in readiness for an all out attack. Hitler issued his war Directive No 25 in which he stated that 'the ground installations of the Yugoslav Air Force and the city of Belgrade will be destroyed from the air by continual night and day attack.' In the Ionian, Adriatic and Aegean Seas, the Italian and British navies had already locked horns, and in the battle of Matapan off the southernmost point of Greece, aided by interception of top secret Italian communications, the British wiped out five out of eight Italian cruisers and three out of thirteen destroyers. Two and a half thousand Italian sailors were drowned. (One of the Royal Navy Midshipmen in the battle was the Greek Prince Philip, who was mentioned in despatches for his work directing searchlights against enemy aircraft.)

With the amassing of enemy aircraft to the north there was considerable fear that the Germans were about to launch an airborne invasion of Greece. Herford was therefore required to carry a loaded revolver for the first time. He doubted whether he could ever use it.

As the prospect of conflict came closer to reality the by-word suddenly became 'security' and a state of alert was declared, German paratroopers were fully expected to fill the skies at any moment. But even an army on full alert was prone to the most basic errors. A Corporal from the Intelligence Corps sprung a surprise visit on Herford's unit to test their security arrangements; they challenged him to produce his identity card, but to their triumphant glee he was unable to do so, and slid away with his tail between his legs.

For another week life at Larissa remained carefree. Being stationed in beautiful, undulating countryside was not unlike being on a summer camp. Herford found himself distinctly underworked and had time to roam the surrounding hillsides and prospect bathing sites in occasional pools filled by the clear mountain streams. There was sporadic news of the German attack on Yugoslavia only several hundred miles to the north, but it might have been coming from a different world.

On 6 April the Yugoslav capital, Belgrade, was subjected to a sudden and violent bombing raid. In that day, 17,000 were killed, the highest number of civilian casualties on any one day so far in the war. The massacre was made all the more acute by the fact that the city was filled with thousands of visitors from the countryside who had come to celebrate Palm Sunday. At the same time, each of Yugoslavia's air fields was savagely attacked, and all but a few of its aircraft destroyed. The country felt the full brutal force of the Blitzkrieg, and was brought almost instantly to its knees.

On the same day a German army drove swiftly south from Bulgaria and attacked and captured the northern Greek port of

Salonica. The port of Piraeus, just outside Athens, was bombed by the Luftwaffe, and several Allied merchant ships destroyed. Havoc was caused over a wide area when the 'Clan Fraser', a ship laden with two hundred tons of explosives, suffered a direct hit – that single explosion caused the loss of ten nearby vessels.

News of the attack on Piraeus harbour reached Herford's unit the following day. He was immediately posted to join the staff of the No 81 Base Sub-Area at Larissa, under the command of Colonel Alexander and his second in command, Major Traill. No 81 should have had a staff of eight officers, but Herford was the only one, and he was still only six weeks into his military career. He was given the task of liaison officer with all the medical units in the area. The generic title 'liaison', gives little clue to the exact nature of the duties involved. Herford's job was not to practice medicine, but to communicate with the forward ambulance units and casualty clearing stations, and with the hospitals behind lines to ensure that the forward units were adequately stocked with medicines and general supplies; and to ensure that casualties who required more than superficial treatment were removed quickly to safety.

A map of the outlying units was provided by Colonel Baldwin of the Signals Regiment, but it gave only scanty details of their locations. The job of accurately plotting their whereabouts was made all the more difficult by the woeful inadequacy of Greek maps, which were at best sketchy, and omitted a lot of important detail. Herford could not work adequately from the map, so decided that the only sensible course was to get his bearings by visiting the ambulance units in person. The only available transport was a motorcycle, so he made the best use of it, and took his first motorcycle ride in thirteen years.

Herford spent the next five days visiting the outlying units on his motorcycle. The Greek roads were perilous, winding and badly pot-holed. These journeys were uncomfortable and exhausting but necessary if the lines of communication were to be kept open. In mountainous country, radios could not always be relied upon.

The fighting had still not spread as far south as Larissa, but the Germans captured Thessalonika in the north, and had quickly advanced as far south as the Aliakmon line (so-called after the river Aliakmon running across north-eastern Greece), 50 miles to the north of Larissa. The Greek army was putting up a spirited defence, but they had been at close grips with a better equipped foe for some time, and the Germans were rapidly punching holes in their thinning defences.

On 12 April Herford rode the forty or so miles north east to Kalabaka near the town of Grevena in search of the 168 Light Field Ambulance Unit. He found chaos and disorganisation in the face of a harsh German assault. He met a Major whose unit had been some ten miles further north in the Grevna pass but which had come under relentless fire. Not having nearly enough men or firepower to resist, they retreated rapidly, laying mines as they went, which would do no more than impede German progress for a short while until an Australian unit came forward to reinforce them. He was disspirited and pessimistic. Even with reinforcements the enemy advance could only be delayed.

Herford pushed the motorcycle hard on the return journey. It was clear that the invasion force pushing down from the north could not be held off for long and that casualties were going to be high. The Enfield 250 engine was doing sterling service, pulling up the steepest hills, but it was built more for speed than agility and the relatively smooth British roads. Every time the front tyre smacked into a pothole the front suspension clanged as the springs reached their full compression, causing the rider to lurch dangerously forward, and calling upon all his reserves of courage to hold on. Herford managed one near-miss after another, but on a straight stretch he hit an unexpected pot-hole, fought to regain control, but smashed into a second. The combined impact snapped the steering column in two and sent him and the bike skittering across the gravelly road.

Badly shaken, but mercifully still in one piece, he was forced to push his wounded machine along the side of the road until the driver of a supply lorry kindly stopped and gave him and his bike a ride to the nearest unit. Luckily there was an efficient motor workshop attached which managed to effect a rapid repair. They carried spare parts for most service vehicles, but also had lathes and spare steel rods which were skilfully employed by craftsmen mechanics to make new components. Herford was back on his bike by early evening and returned to his unit by nightfall.

By 14 April it was clear that they were only days from being overrun. The Germans had broken through the Aliakmon line at several key points and were channelling their forces through under the cover of heavy fire and aerial bombardment. Some of the Greek soldiers became so disgusted with the way that their defences had been organised that they fired on their own officers.

Herford was told by Colonel Alexander that an ambulance train was being sent to Pharsala, some 40 miles to the south, to aid the speedy evacuation of the mounting casualties. The boom of heavy gunfire and distant crack of rifles could now be clearly heard. In the space of three days the peaceful, pastoral landscape only a few miles up country had become a bloody battle field. Alexander took the view that it was no longer a question of whether they could supply sufficient blankets to the casualty clearing stations, but whether they could get the wounded away before they fell into enemy hands. There was a distinct possibility that Lt Colonel Mollan, the Commanding Officer of 24 CCS and 189 Light Field Ambulance, which were both still stationed ten miles to the west of Larissa, might have to wait and be captured with the wounded who could not be moved.

Herford immediately rode out to see Colonel Mollan's HQ and put him in the picture. He stoically accepted Alexander's message and carried on tending to the wounded that were being ferried back from the front. The casualty clearing station was at full stretch, its tented operating theatre and ward were at capacity. The surgeons worked sixteen hours a day removing shrapnel and bullets, cauterising, suturing and even amputating under the most basic conditions.

Herford paid a similar visit to 24 Casualty Clearing Station, where they were kind enough to let him borrow their Austin motor car. He travelled quickly south to Pharsala, where he had instructions to order the New Zealand field hospital to evacuate all casualties on the ambulance train. Herford left Larissa at midnight, calling at the Medical Inspection (MI) room at Headquarters to see that everything was still in order and to let them know that he would be back the following morning.

Fighting exhaustion, Herford arrived in Pharsala at 4 a.m. The situation was in disarray; three hundred patients had been taken to the station, loaded onto the train and then unloaded, because the order came back that the train was for the evacuation of wounded Greek soldiers only. Incensed, he finally succeeded in having the goods wagons unloaded, but on returning to the hospital at 8 a.m. he found that another order had been radioed through in the interim instructing all personnel to abandon camp and withdraw to Athens at once. The staff were busy loading casualties and equipment into trucks.

Herford heard that another ambulance train had meanwhile made it up to Larissa, so he returned to organise its loading. During the drive he wondered whether there would still be a station when he arrived. German planes were rumbling overhead and half way along the road he encountered several British lorries burning fiercely at the roadside, victims of German fighters who had swooped down low and caught them with strafing fire.

As he neared Larissa he could see the puffs of black smoke being thrown into the air by exploding shells. The town was being sporadically bombarded from the north. Fortunately he did not encounter any fighter aircraft on the final stretch, and made it to the station unscathed. Mortars were landing nearby and the Greek railway staff had vanished. The platforms were crowded with both walking wounded and stretcher cases. Eventually the train pulled into the station, and the injured were quickly loaded on board. In spite of the fire raining down on the town, the train pulled out without being hit and carried 177 men southwards to safety.

Herford went immediately from the station to Headquarters, but found it as eerily deserted as the *Marie Celeste*. Overnight all the remaining stores and personnel had been cleared out and evacuated south to Pharsala; the Germans were now only a few miles away to the north.

At midnight Herford set off again for Pharsala, but the roads were completely jammed with military vehicles retreating south, and heavy rain was washing streams of mud onto the tarmac reducing it to a sticky quagmire. He waited two hours in a traffic jam making no progress. He had a choice – either to spend another sleepless night stuck in a sitting-duck queue, or to return to Larissa for some sleep and hope that the Germans didn't arrive before morning. He calculated the odds were even either way; he was dog-tired so took the latter course.

After a few hours of fretful sleep in the deserted HQ, he was woken at dawn by the sound of bombing and machine gun fire alarmingly close to the camp. He jumped back in the Austin and headed south on the now clear road for Pharsala. Tracer bullets were streaking through the half light of the dawn, making a strangely attractive sight.

There were even more smouldering wrecks of lorries at the roadside than there had been the day before, and the fighter planes were increasing in activity. Herford put his boot to the boards and pushed the little car along as fast as he could given the treacherous conditions, but his heart leapt into his mouth as German bombers suddenly appeared over the crest of a hill and screamed overhead. Driving on was foolhardy – pilots loved a moving target. Herford screeched to a halt and ran to the side of the road, taking cover in a shallow ditch. The planes droned overhead and released their deadly payload. The ground shook with the impact of the explosion and a hail of flying earth and metal fragments whistled over the top of the ditch, but he emerged unscathed – and so did the Austin!

Herford found Colonel Alexander in Pharsala preparing to leave with Major Traill for Thebes, from where they were to be evacuated from the country. Alexander asked Herford to come with them, but he refused, requesting to continue his liaison work for as long as possible. Alexander thanked him profoundly, saying that if there were as many officers as dedicated to their duty much of the chaos which was now occurring could have been avoided. Herford was still very much concerned with the fate of 24 CCS and 189 LFA, whom he had learned were still in situ at Larissa, which was under fire, but still holding out against the Germans. Alexander said that the medical staff would simply have to stay and be captured. This was the normal military practice, and ensured that casualties who were seized by the enemy would be given adequate treatment. Herford suggested that they might adopt the policy employed at Dunkirk, whereby one MO and two orderlies were left behind each with 100 men. Alexander agreed that this course of action should be taken.

Herford made the trip to 24 CCS and 189 LFA by-passing Larissa. He reached Colonel Mollan in time to look along the valley and watch Larissa disappearing under a merciless barrage of bombs. The Germans were only ten miles away, but there was still time to stage a speedy evacuation. Mollan assumed it was his duty to remain and be captured with the casualties who could not be moved, but Herford told him that Alexander had approved the Dunkirk plan. Losing no time, the casualties were loaded into ambulances and a convoy transporting 176 wounded left the camp site leaving behind most of the medical equipment with a handful of staff and the unfortunate wounded who were too ill to transport. Herford resorted to his trusted motorcycle and led the convoy.

They moved south to Pharsala in torrential rains and arrived safely at the now abandoned New Zealand hospital site. Most of the equipment which had been left behind had been looted, and only the tentage and a few immovable items remained. It was decided to hole up for a few hours, but soon after they arrived German bombers descended. A salvo of bombs was released only yards from the field hospital. Most personnel were afforded some shelter in the slit trenches, and one bomb dropped only 30 yards away, sending showers of earth and stones over their heads.

Colonel Mollan decided it was far too risky to stay and ordered the column to proceed to Levadia, which was another 70 miles to the south. Herford again rode at the front on the motorcycle. Lack of sleep was catching up with him and as they proceeded slowly up the Lamia Pass, travelling no faster then ten miles per hour, he felt his eyes forcing themselves together, as if being dragged down by lead weights. When they reached the top of the pass Herford could go no further and was forced to stop for a few hours sleep while the convoy continued on. He decided that they had come far enough south to be safe from German fire, so he made a 'bed' at the roadside and spent a few fitful hours staving off the cold and dozing restlessly.

He awoke at dawn beneath a clear blue sky. All was silence, except for the chirps of a few hardy songbirds. He felt like the returning Odysseus lying on a mossy bed with a pillow of stone. The view from his lofty perch was almost magical. For a few precious moments war seemed an eternity away. The valley spread out beneath him in full spring bloom. The road wound and coiled down the craggy slopes. At the top there was nothing but scrub and rock and the occasional fir tree, defying the elements and drawing its nutrition from an unknown source. Lower down the scrub became more dense, the trees more numerous, until in the upper reaches of the valley the green of the firs merged with the pink almond blossoms; these in turn yielded to the deep ochre of the ploughed fields at the valley bottom, interspersed with little hamlets of white-washed houses. He cherished these moments of peace, and soaked in this entrancing view before shattering the calm with the roar of his motorcycle engine.

Herford caught up with the convoy 15 miles to the south outside Amphikia, where they had pitched camp. He spent the day planning a bigger evacuation of casualties from surrounding units, and liaised with Colonel Johnston of the 2/7 Australian MDS. Herford raised the possibility of bringing an ambulance train up to the town of Levadia, some 20 miles to the south, which could carry most of the wounded back to Athens. Johnston thought it an attractive idea, but was pessimistic as to the chances of success. All available transport was being thrown into service in a full scale retreat.

Herford had the advantage of still being a new boy in the army with comparatively little understanding of the sensitivity of relationships between officers. Still less did he appreciate that the military machinery was capable of operating in the most bureaucratic way, even in the direst of circumstances. He grabbed the nearest field telephone and phoned through to the Rail Transport Officer in Athens and demanded an ambulance train be sent up the line by dawn. The Transport Officer was predictably reluctant, saying that there were far too many calls on their rolling stock already. Outraged by this apparent indifference to a parlous situation, Herford demanded to speak to the Senior Officer. When an equally officious Major came on the line Herford struck a haughty tone, and said he was acting on the direct instructions of Colonel Alexander. (Herford had no idea where Alexander was, but was sure that he would have given the order he was now making on his behalf). The Major took some convincing, and during this conversation Colonel Bellisario of the 2/7 Australian

Casualty Clearing Station came into the room and listened in. Herford felt distinctly uneasy about continuing his subterfuge in the presence of a Colonel, but when finally the Major backed down, Bellisario laughed out loud, clapped him on the back and thanked him profusely. Herford had been in the army less than two months and had already managed to assume the authority of a full Colonel.

The following day 24 CCS moved their camp next to 2/3 Australian CCS just outside Levadia. They suddenly found themselves busy as trains pulling goods wagons loaded with wounded arrived from the north. Herford organised the details of orderlies who unloaded the stretcher cases and ferried them to the Casualty Clearing Stations for treatment. It was tiring work, and his extreme lack of sleep was beginning to catch up with him. As soon as the last wagon was unloaded he returned to camp, had a simple meal and fell into a deep sleep.

He awoke at dawn the following morning to the sound of heavy bombing several miles away. He rushed out of his tent to see Levadia receiving the full force of a German air raid. The station, which the day before had been the scene of intense activity, was reduced to a mass of rubble. A massive explosion split the air as a nearby ammunition dump was hit. Another bomb hit an RAF fuel dump, and 50,000 gallons of fuel instantly leapt into flame. The dawn sky was illuminated with a swirling scarlet fireball, followed by a dense black column of smoke which seemed to rise hundreds of feet into the windless air. It was still before reveille but the camp was already bursting into activity. Herford hurriedly dressed and shaved, expecting more casualties, when the air was suddenly filled with the high-pitched whine of German fighter planes. They descended low over the camp spitting out several hundred rounds of ammunition as they passed, sending personnel scattering and diving for cover. No sooner had Herford got back to his feet after the first fly-past, than the fighters circled back round and continued strafing the road and anyone and anything that happened to be in their path. By this method maximum disruption could be caused to the military transport, and a good deal of panic instilled those on the ground. To many of the men, including Herford, dodging fighter planes was a new and horrifying experience, and engendered a complete sense of helplessness as they descended like a cloud of lethal hornets.

When the aircraft activity died down, Herford received a message that an ambulance train was coming up the line to Thebes, 30 miles to the south, and he was required to organise the removal of casualties. Transport was severely limited, so he had no option but to resort once again to the motorcycle.

Travelling along damaged roads on two wheels was a mixed blessing. Primitive suspension and a hard leather saddle made for an uncomfortable ride, but Herford was able to jump off quickly and dive for cover during the sporadic swoops along the road by fighter aircraft. All thoughts of the beauty of the Greek spring had now been supplanted by far more pressing concerns. Simply getting to Thebes in one piece required total concentration. Apart from the danger presented by air attacks, the other vehicles on the road were driving in an extremely hazardous manner. The Greeks were temperamental drivers at the best of times, but with the added threat of air attack they drove at full pelt, in the hope that by shortening their journey time they would lessen the chances of being hit. Herford soon observed that this had the reverse effect. Fast moving vehicles attracted fire, and when they came under attack the driver would invariably lose control and plough off the road. The road to Thebes was littered with burning and smouldering wrecks, some no doubt still containing the charred remains of their unfortunate drivers.

He made steady progress, and was constantly alert to the expressions of the Greeks at the roadside. He couldn't hear the distant sound of an aircraft over the noise of his motorcycle, but when others suddenly darted into their houses he knew it was time to quit the road. But near Thebes the situation worsened. The town and the surrounding area was under heavy aerial attack. Several sections of the road were cratered and rendered virtually impassable by the small bombs dropped from Dorniers. So engrossed was he in negotiating the hazards in his path that an approaching Dornier took him completely by surprise. The plane suddenly appeared over a hill and skimmed the road. Herford was the only moving object in sight, and to the pilot must have looked like little more than an ant. Herford uttered a silent prayer, but was suddenly shaken by the penetrating crack of a bomb erupting on the road behind him. Miraculously it was far enough behind to have left him unharmed. Instinctively he wrenched on the throttle, but another bomb dropped some thirty yards ahead of him. It was too late to take evasive action. He felt the hot blast of the explosion and was catapulted from the motorcycle into the dust and earth clear of the road.

For what seemed like minutes he lay motionless, waiting for a searing pain, too frightened to move a muscle. But gradually he started to move each limb in turn, and to his astonishment found he was completely unhurt. The bomb had landed just off the tarmacadam and had sunk straight into the soft ground at the roadside. It had thrown up a sizeable mound of soil, but the earth had absorbed the majority of the blast and the shrapnel. Herford apprehensively checked the sky, and waited several minutes before venturing out into the open again. The Dornier did not return. The pilot must have flown off happily congratulating himself on scoring a direct hit.

By a minor miracle the motorcycle was virtually undamaged and started with no hitches. Herford was not a fatalist, and acutely aware that common sense and keeping a cool head was the best protection from accidents, but he was now beginning to wonder just how long his good luck would last. Having escaped with barely a scratch it felt almost churlish to tempt fate again but he drove into Thebes in the middle of an air raid.

The moral duty of a doctor at war, to put the safety of his patients above that of his own, is virtually absolute. It is alarming enough for the able-bodied to be caught in a hail of exploding bombs, but far more traumatic to those who are totally reliant on others for their well-being. As Herford weaved through the streets towards the railway station, he knew that one of the prime objectives for the bombers would be the railway track and rolling stock. It was imperative to get the ambulance train out as quickly as possible. Once it was underway it was hoped that the red crosses on the wagon roofs would prevent it from being shot at, but the track itself was a legitimate target.

The station was already the scene of intense, but disorganised activity. Stretcher cases had been unloaded from ambulances and placed in the ambulance train, but the carriages had been repeatedly hit by strafing bullets and nearly all the windows were shattered. Reports also came in that the track had been cut five miles down the line towards Athens.

Herford's first priority was to help in giving first aid to those who had been wounded in the air raids. Despite the repeated air attacks morale still remained high among the wounded, some of whom were cracking jokes and making the others laugh. When the situation was that tense laughter was often a natural reaction, and the most effective defence mechanism.

It was obvious that the ambulance train could no longer be sent out, so Herford sent a radio message to the nearby Force Headquarters and requested a fleet of ambulances to evacuate the train. He organised details to begin removing the stretchers to the platform while they awaited transport. While he was carrying one casualty out he saw a Sergeant jump onto a motorcycle just outside the station and roar away – then he realised it was *his* motorcycle. His next major concern was the train itself. There were only a handful of ambulance trains in the whole of Greece, so it was vitally important to save it if at all possible. At present it was not yet coupled to an engine, and two out of three available locomotives had suffered considerable bomb damage. The lines near the station were also clogged with wagons. Herford found an engine which appeared to be intact and went in search of a driver. The Greek railway staff were extremely reluctant to emerge from cover, so Herford was forced to chase one out with a rifle. The driver was persuaded to help clear the lines by shunting the wagons clear. Herford observed closely and took to the controls to do some of the driving himself.

As the track was being cleared bombs continued to drop into the area. Herford was so engrossed in his work shunting the engine and using the gradient to move rolling stock clear that he was able to close his mind from the danger. But at one stage they were just clear of the station when four Meschersmidts came down low, shot up four lorries at the edge of the track and then made a bee-line for the engine.

Herford hit the deck but the plane passed over without firing. He looked up to see the train driver smugly grinning back at him!

When finally the line had been cleared he returned to the ambulance wagons and found that they had nearly been cleared, and the casualties removed by road. Only Captain Simmonds, the MO of the ambulance train, remained. Simmonds was as anxious as Herford that the train be saved, so together with a Greek driver and mate, they took the train 'out of town'. Just as they were pulling out of the station another strafe began, and a bomb thumped down to the ground where only moments previously the engine had been standing. The train continued through the suburbs and into the country beyond. For a while it seemed as if the air raids had died down, but suddenly a pack of bombers appeared over the horizon making straight for them. As they got closer the driver panicked. Herford urged him on but his fear got the better of him. He brought the engine to a screeching halt and he and his mate sprinted for cover. Herford and Simmonds crossed their fingers as the distant drone became a deafening roar – then faded gradually away as they continued on to more important targets.

Having spent several fretful hours on the footplate with the irascible driver Herford felt it was time to get his own back. Before the driver and his mate emerged, he started up the engine and began to pull away without them. The two Greeks appeared from the undergrowth, and had to break the record for the mile to catch up!

They brought the train to a halt close to the break in the line and left it in the hope that the track would shortly be repaired. Herford and Simmonds walked the four miles back to Headquarters and got their hands on some much needed refreshment. Herford was anxious to return to 24 CCS at Levadia as casualties were still coming in thick and fast, but there was neither a car nor a motorcycle to be had. He would have to bed down for the night in the hope of getting up to Levadia in the morning. But before he could succumb to sleep he was called to tend to a wounded German pilot who had been shot down that afternoon. Herford administered first aid to the man's superficial injuries and travelled with him in a truck to 168 Light Field Ambulance where he received the same treatment as any British soldier. Herford got hold of a blanket from the ambulance stores, found a spare camp bed and finally lay down at 2 a.m.

The 168 LFA breakfasted anxiously at dawn. Everyone was jittery as their camp had been bombed the previous day and their surgeon killed. They counted themselves extremely lucky that they had lost no one else. Poor communications and desperate shortage of transport was making them ever more gloomy about the prospect of effecting a successful evacuation.

Herford had to work quickly if they were not to be captured. Ordinary soldiers could make a run for it in any way they could, but medical staff could retreat only as quickly as they could bring their most seriously wounded with them. He scouted around the units in the area until he managed to secure the loan of another motorcycle and made for Levadia to discuss evacuation plans with Colonel Johnston. To his amazement he found Johnston in complete ignorance of any plans for a widespread evacuation of casualties. Exasperated, Herford had no choice but to return to Thebes to see what progress was being made in repairing the railway track.

The Greeks had moved with startling efficiency, and a gang of navvies were already busy heaving new sleepers and girders into place, but it would take the rest of the day before it was fit for use. Heartened, Herford returned to Levadia and with Colonel Johnston's assistance set about organising an ambulance column which would move out the following day.

Shortly after darkness fell Colonel Bellisario of 24 CCS ordered a complete evacuation. Over 200 patients were loaded into a convoy of ambulances together with a large quantity of equipment, and they moved slowly down the road to a small station outside Thebes which Herford had reconnoitred the previous day. This time there were no hitches; the train was loaded successfully and made its way back to Athens.

Herford turned around straight away and was back at Headquarters by dawn on 23 April to receive a welcome mail parcel containing letters from his brother Harold in India and from his sister, Sylvia, both of whom had new babies. Reading these welcome communications he felt a tinge of guilt, both because his mind was so occupied with immediate concerns that he had not been able to write, and also because in the thick of action he found it difficult to share in their joy.

Colonel Johnston outlined detailed plans for the evacuation of the entire Allied force from Greece, codename Operation Demon. The whole expedition had been an unmitigated disaster – the object of the exercise was now to decamp as quickly as possible losing as few men as possible. For the time being at least, Herford did not have to play an organisational role, and was able to pack up his kit and get ready for departure to Athens that evening. He loaded his motorcycle into the back of a 3 ton truck, cleared a space amidst the stacks of equipment to lie down in and slept for most of the journey.

That same day the Greek Army surrendered to the Germans. The Greeks had lost several thousand soldiers, the Allies more than 900. The Greeks were bereft. The tragedy of the situation was summed up in one incident which occurred when Major Versis of the Greek Artillery was ordered to surrender his guns. While his men sung the national anthem he ceremonially shot himself through the head.

Herford awoke at dawn on the morning of 24 April to find that the truck had overshot Athens by nearly 40 miles and was nearly at Megara, one of the embarkation points for the evacuating troops. He banged on the cab and made the driver stop. He had been ordered to report to Brigadier Large, the Director Medical Services in Greece, who was based in the capital. Herford unloaded his motorcycle and cursing himself set off back along the road, negotiating the numerous wrecked military and civilian vehicles at the roadside and no less than 56 dead mules, all of which had been mercilessly machine gunned by fighter planes.

He was greeted at Brigadier Large's office with exclamations of 'Oh, so you're the man everyone is talking about.' He learned that Lt Colonel Mollan's evacuation with 189 LFA and 24 CCS had been subject to some investigation, and Herford was asked to confirm Colonel Alexander's evacuation orders in writing. Herford duly obliged, and later found out from Mollan that he had saved him from a court martial for failing to remain with his unit to await capture. Herford was able to confirm Alexander's order that the Dunkirk plan be adopted.

Brigadier Large then asked, 'Can you drive a lorry? Because there is something I want done very urgently.'

Herford gave a distinctly dubious 'Yes'. He had a little experience in Spain, but the Greek roads demanded more than superficial skills.

Large explained that he simply didn't have any drivers available. The Navy was concerned that the evacuation wasn't going to happen as quickly as they had hoped. Any delay would probably result in several battles taking place in the Peloponnese. There was a dire shortage of medical equipment, so someone was required to drive a three-toner loaded up with supplies from the Base Medical Stores down to the port of Argos, some 150 miles to the South West. The objective was to get the stores to 189 LFA, or otherwise to distribute them as best he could among the medical units.

Brigadier Large telephoned for the lorry, and with no instruction Herford was told to get on with the job. Minutes later he loaded his motorcycle into the back of an empty three-toner and climbed tentatively behind the wheel of what felt like a double-decker bus and gingerly eased the growling diesel engine into gear. Picking his way careful amidst the reckless pedestrians and trams, he managed to find his way to 26th General Hospital where he was to load up with supplies. But venturing inside he found that most of the staff had already been evacuated, and the rest were rushed off their feet preparing for the removal of the more serious cases. The supplies he required were up on the fourth floor, and it was simply impossible for one man to load them unaided. But there was no alternative but to at least make a start on the job. As he was loading the truck he noticed two young Greek men and two women peering over the railings at him, their curiosity aroused by the boxes of supplies. Herford called them in and enlisted their help loading up. He rewarded them with blankets, but after they left he suddenly regretted not having offered them whatever they wanted. They were shortly to be occupied by an invading German army, and months, if not years of even greater hardship were bound to follow.

With the lorry well and truly laden down, Herford set off on his journey. With all the added weight in the rear it now felt like steering a ship, and driving took immense concentration.

Having travelled some hours and overcome with hunger and fatigue, he pulled up at a small roadside taverna to buy some food to eat en route. As he waited at the back of the restaurant he sensed the acute difference between his pressing mission and the relatively relaxed atmosphere amongst the diners here, carrying on almost as normal. Their country had effectively surrendered to an aggressor, and now they had little to do except sit and wait for the Germans to arrive. He sat alone in the corner, a young, square-jawed English officer wearing an ever so slightly anxious expression, which gave him a permanent look of concern.

A few minutes later a waiter approached with a note. Mystified, Herford unfolded it, and read that the author wished to see him in the cloakroom. Cautiously he rose to his feet and made his way around the corner and along the passage out of view of the main dining room. Waiting for him there was a brown-eyed, olive-skinned Greek girl. He asked a little shyly if she was the author of the note. She replied that she was, her voice trembling slightly. She was extremely pretty, and he could tell from her expression that she was barely containing her distress.

She spoke in faltering English, 'Please, I need to leave Greece. I am desperate,' she pleaded, 'Take me with you. You could smuggle me out with the British troops. Please –'

Herford felt a surge of compassion well within him, but he knew it was out of the question. He would have taken her if he could, but to what? Every man and item of equipment loaded on board the evacuation craft would be checked and accounted for. He would only be leading her into trouble as well as himself.

He tried to explain that he couldn't take her. The girl listened, fighting back her disappointment. She left him without crying, but he was in no doubt that she was merely saving her tears from him. He left the restaurant with a heavy heart, wondering what would become of the beautiful young woman under the Nazi yoke.

It was late afternoon when Herford pulled away on the second leg of his journey to Argos. A little distance along the road he stopped to pick up a solitary Australian soldier who had become separated from his unit and wanted to get to Argos. A second pair of eyes in the cab was extremely useful for spotting enemy aircraft. As they drew closer to their destination there were increasing numbers of burning vehicles at the side of the road. Several times German bombers came in overhead, but each time they were bound elsewhere or had already discharged their cargo. The chief objective seemed to be destroying the means of escape, and Herford witnessed several planes attacking a number of small boats just off the coast, only several hundred yards from the road.

As darkness fell they were more than two thirds of the way to their destination. They passed another group of soldiers who were also thumbing a lift, so Herford let them jump on board. Progress was tortuously slow as the narrow road was winding and hilly, and a strict blackout was enforced. He could drive no faster than a snail's pace. At one stage they passed 24 CCS at the roadside. Their train had been bombed and they were waiting for transport. The three-ton truck was already at full capacity, so Herford was unable to offer them a lift.

They crawled into Argos at midnight. The passengers bid Herford farewell and left for the nearby port of Naphplion, the main evacuation point in the area. Herford scoured the town for an HQ or information post but could find nothing which looked even vaguely like an administrative centre. He was wandering like a lost soul when he was approached by an excitable Greek policeman who asked in broken English if he was an English officer. When Herford answered that he was, the policeman led him quickly back through the blackout to a police station where there was an urgent telephone call waiting.

At the other end was a Captain Rose, who had been trying all day to get hold of Brigadier Lee, who was meant to be in charge of the evacuation at Argos, but the Brigadier was nowhere to be found. Rose was running out of patience. He had an urgent message from the Commander in Chief of the Mediterranean forces concerning a change in the evacuation plans. It was vitally important that it be communicated to someone in authority. He pleaded with Herford to go out and find an operational officer who could take the message.

The only thing Herford could do was to stop staff cars at random which were interspersed in the convoys of troop carriers passing through the town. After several unsuccessful attempts to interest passing officers in the message he stopped two Brigadiers who immediately went to take the message from Rose. Herford overheard the conversation, and was left in no doubt that the situation had descended into a shambles and was 'going blind.' There was a complete absence of central organisation in the troop movements, and things had almost descended to the level where it was every man for himself.

Still needing to find a competent officer to advise him on the distribution of his lorry load of supplies, he continued to wave down staff cars in the hope of finding someone who was vaguely willing to assume authority. To his surprise he stopped a car containing Colonel Alexander and Major Traill. They had just come in from Athens on their way to Naphplion.

Alexander had not heard anything about expected battles in the Pellopanese, and fully expected the evacuation to be completed within two days. There seemed to be an almost total lack of communication between senior officers, a fact which reinforced in Herford's mind the view he had already formed – that the backbone of an army is its lines of communications. Colonel Alexander was unable to help with the whereabouts of 189 LFA, and advised him to leave the supplies with a Greek hospital and get himself evacuated at once.

Herford was not content simply to off-load his responsibility, and continued intercepting staff cars until he met Colonel Baldwin of 81 Base Sub Area who had with him two 15 cwt signals trucks. Baldwin suggested he follow him to Kalamata, a major embarkation point some 150 miles south west where the stores would be greatly appreciated.

Herford dutifully joined the little convoy and negotiated yet more tortuous mountain roads for the rest of the night. By dawn he could no longer keep his eyes open, and simply fell asleep at one of their halts. One of the signals drivers offered to relieve him for a while, and Herford gratefully accepted the opportunity for a nap in the passenger seat. But within half an hour the driver lost control of the truck and ditched it irretrievably.

The signalmen off loaded some of the stores onto their lorries, but extricating the three-toner was out of the question. One of them agreed to stay behind while the others proceeded to Kalamata. Herford retrieved his motorbike and went to see if he could find transport which could carry his supplies to their destination. He returned unsuccessful several hours later, only to find that his companion had allowed passing Greeks to take what they wanted from the stranded lorry! Herford was extremely angry, and decided that he would have to guard it himself in the hope that one of the passing vehicles would be sufficiently empty to load up his supplies. But as he waited tiredness overcame him again, and in his moments of sleep locals descended as if from nowhere and helped themselves.

Fortunately one of the passing staff cars contained Colonel Jasper Blunt, the British Military Attaché in Greece. He posted his driver to guard the lorry and took Herford down to his HQ in Tripolis from where he later sent back a truck to collect the remaining stores. This was a welcome meeting – in Tripolis Herford had a wash, shave, some food and a few hours' much needed rest.

Determined to see his job through, Herford climbed back on board his motorcycle and drove from Tripolis to Kalamata to oversee the distribution of the supplies ferried there by the signalmen. Not surprisingly, Kalamata was the scene of considerable chaos. The olive groves were filled with English, Australian and New Zealand soldiers, but the HQ was nowhere to be found. The signalmen were meant to be co-ordinating the communications for the evacuation, but even they had no idea what was happening. Herford sought out a Greek hospital and gave them his supplies, which were gratefully received. It seemed to be the only organised medical facility in the entire area.

He passed an uncomfortable night camping with some Australian soldiers in an olive grove before returning to Tripolis the following day. The road was jammed with troop carriers, but fortunately there were no air raids, otherwise they would have been sitting ducks. Twice Herford had to stop to administer first aid; once to a Greek driver whose lorry had been machine gunned, and once to an Australian Sergeant who had struck a match while sitting on a petrol can in the back of a truck, giving himself severe burns.

On his return to Tripolis, he went at Colonel Blunt's suggestion to the Tripolis hospital to drop off some of his bulkier supplies. There he visited a number of severely wounded British soldiers who were too ill to be moved. They were desperately anxious to be evacuated, but when it was explained to them that it was simply impossible they accepted stoically and without protest. At this time the foremost German troops were only several miles to the north. The New Zealanders had taken up the rear-guard position just outside Tripolis and would hold off the enemy until the following day when it was hoped the evacuation would be completed.

Herford made his final journey in Greece overnight with the help of a Greek guide who led him and Captain Fisher, an MO, the 150 miles south from Tripolis to Monemvasia, a small port on the southernmost tip of the Pellopanese. Here he stashed the remainder of the supplies in a medical hut, for use by any troops bringing up the rear, although he himself was very near the tail-end of the evacuation. He was due to leave that evening in a caique with Colonel Blunt and a party of other officers. For the rest of the day he lay low. There was considerable bombing, but of the kind specifically designed to draw fire and pin-point concentrations of Allied troops. In the far distance could be heard much heavy bombing coming from Naphplion. One of the British ships in the harbour, SS *Slammat*, was overloaded with troops when it was struck by a direct hit. Two escort ships, HMS *Wryneck* and HMS *Diamond* picked up many of those from the foundering ship, but both were then sunk with further direct hits with almost total loss of life. They had run our of ammunition. Herford was extremely grateful that he had persisted with his distribution of medical supplies, otherwise he might well have been one of those killed in the Naphplion evacuations.

Colonel Blunt's party gathered on the shore at dusk and waited anxiously for the arrival of the caique. It was several hours late, and for a time they wondered whether the Germans would arrive before their boat, but eventually through the darkness came the reassuring chug-chug of the diesel engine.

Fifteen men boarded the tiny vessel together with a quantity of medical supplies, and set off across the choppy sea to the small island of Kythera. Herford and Blunt sat at the bow, a groundsheet spread over their knees to keep off the spray. The little boat bobbed up and down erratically, its engine whirring noisily when it crested a high wave, but the boatman handled his craft expertly, even with such a heavy pay load.

Herford produced a medical water bottle of fine rum from an abandoned RAF lorry, which helped to pass the time and keep out the cold from the keen wind. Under the cloak of night they were safe from enemy aircraft and could enjoy a few carefree hours after so many days of high drama. Herford and Blunt had much in common and their conversation ran freely from the Greek campaign to philosophy and the future of Europe. Blunt was widely travelled. He knew India and the Far East. He was an expert falconer.

The caique reached the shores of Kythera at dawn, where the party spent the day before being collected by a Navy cruiser later that night. Never one to let the opportunity of climbing a mountain pass by, Herford spent the day with a New Zealander, Corporal Curd, climbing to the summit of the island where they explored an abandoned monastery, and after the hard climb drank eagerly from a water butt filled with perfectly pure tasting rain water.

The HMS *Auckland* appeared off-shore in the early evening. In a rough swell Herford's party and 750 RAF personnel climbed aboard. The decks were jam-packed, and the crossing to Crete was an uncomfortable one. At Crete Colonel Blunt took most of his party ashore. One of their number, Colonel Quillam, Director of Military Intelligence, Greece, suggested that Herford come on with him to Alexandria, the Auckland's next port of call, and from there back to Cairo. Crete held no particular attraction, so Herford decided the better course was to attempt to rejoin his original unit in Egypt. (At that stage nobody suspected an imminent German invasion of Crete, and the Greek government and King had moved there. Colonel Blunt was to take care of them.)

On the morning of 1 May Herford arrived in a busy Alexandria harbour, from where he took the train to Cairo. Brigadier Large happened to be on the same train, and requested a detailed report of his movements from when he left Athens. Herford conscientiously wrote up his report as soon as he had snatched a few hours' rest in Shepherd's hotel, but it provided little useful information other than that communications generally, and particularly in the medical service, had been extremely poor, bordering on non-existent. Whatever procedures had been in place had crumbled to dust during the retreat.

Herford's blooding in the ill-fated Greek campaign won him his first decoration, the Member of the Order of the British Empire, 'in recognition of distinguished services in the Middle East.' The official citation reads:

> 'This officer was detailed to remain behind with 24 Casualty Clearing Station, to await capture by the enemy, and performed very good service. In addition, he constituted himself liaison officer between this CCS and the Ambulance Trains sent up as often as possible to points varying between 5 and 20 miles from this CCS. When the troops had withdrawn from the CCS area, communication with the CCS ceased, but Lieut. Herford, with the aid of a motorcycle, succeeded in making contact with the ambulance train as it arrived, so facilitating evacuation of casualties from 24 Casualty Clearing Station that it was able to withdraw before capture, having evacuated all its casualties.'

That this citation contains a number of inaccuracies came as no surprise to Herford when he finally saw it for the first time in 1976. Firstly, he was not detailed to remain behind with 24 CCS, but asked to remain behind to act as liaison officer when the other officers in 81 Base Sub-Area withdrew. Secondly, his function was not to liaise between 24 CCS and the ambulance trains. He voluntarily assumed the function of liaising between all the medical units in the area, British and Australian. Thirdly, 24 CCS was able to withdraw before capture not because Herford made contact with the ambulance train, but because, at his suggestion, Colonel Alexander decided to adopt the Dunkirk plan of allowing one MO and 2 orderlies to remain with every 100 casualties who could not be moved. And fourthly, his role in managing the ambulance trains amounted to considerably more than 'making contact.'

The words of the young guardsman on the way to Greece had been truly prophetic. The Greek campaign was one of the most ill-conceived and badly executed of the war, mounted at the last minute and in desperation.

Many of Herford's experiences throughout the following two years in the Western Desert were to do little to alter his tainted view of military organisation.

The Desert War 1941 – 1943

Herford reported to Colonel McFie in Cairo and requested his next posting. He had only been in the army for three months, but had already built a reputation which had preceded him as something of an organiser. It was therefore a little disconcerting when Colonel McFie seemed uncertain what to do with him and simply said, 'Well, what do you want to do next?'

'Anything that's available,' Herford replied.

MacFie consulted the personnel lists on his desk for a minute, then said, 'You can join a Field Ambulance Unit.'

Herford had only an extremely vague idea what the function of a field ambulance was, he was still a military novice and unfamiliar with the jargon.

'Or you can join a motor ambulance convoy,' McFie suggested.

Herford felt foolish, but had to ask what a motor ambulance convoy was. McFie smiled and shook his head. He explained that it consisted of 70 ambulances together with mobile workshop facilities, its task was to provide evacuation facilities for front-line field ambulances. In other words, the convoy's job was to collect casualties and ferry them back to hospitals. The convoy would be commanded by a Major, and Herford would be second in command.

The idea of heading an ambulance convoy which would process across the swirling sands of the Egyptian desert like a latter-day caravan had an instant romantic appeal. Herford had no idea what desert warfare entailed, but he imagined the convoy would provide him with a more independent way of life, which was something he valued above all else. He agreed to take the position, and was posted as 2nd I/C to No 7 Motor Ambulance Convoy.

There were two days before the posting commenced, during which Herford took the rare opportunity to visit the souks of Cairo and write much overdue letters home. Quite by chance, on the final day before collecting his posting papers, he hailed a taxi in the centre of town when a Major stepped smartly out in front of him and bagged it for himself. Herford let out a cry of protest. The Major responded by winding down the window and cheerfully asking him where he was going.

'The Turf Club,' Herford replied.

'So am I,' the grinning Major replied, a cigarette firmly planted between his teeth, and gestured him to jump in.

During a hair-raising journey through the chaotic Cairo traffic, the Major enquired where Herford was posted.

When he told him that he was to join the No 7 MAC the Major looked aghast. 'Good God!' he exclaimed, 'That's my outfit.' He reached across and shook Herford vigorously by the hand, 'I'm Johnny Johnston, your Commanding Officer.'

It was a chance introduction to a charming man who was to become a close friend for the duration of the desert campaign. Johnston has a bright, optimistic view of life which was to do so much to maintain morale in the endless tracts of desert in which they were to lead their nomadic life.

A week later they were posted to Fuka, in the Western Desert. The drive across the white dust roads seemed interminable, and the tents which were their homes afforded little in the way of home comfort; they neither efficiently kept out the bitter cold of the desert nights, nor protected against the relentless heat of the day. What creature comforts there were, were either in the form of tobacco, for those who smoked, or in the prized rations of chocolate, sweets and thick processed cheese, which quickly became a rarity when spending long periods away from base.

Several things were immediately striking about the desert and the strange war which was being acted out, rather than fought, within it. Firstly, when they arrived in the late spring, the monotony of the limitless sand was occasionally broken by vast areas of night scented stock. It seemed to burst into bloom the instant there was a drop of rain, filling the air with an almost magical scent. The contrast between this fragrant perfume and the aridity of the climate was so unexpected as to be almost disconcerting. Secondly, the war seemed almost swallowed up in the vastness of the environment. The pockets of conflict were small and relatively isolated. If battles had to be fought at all, the desert seemed the least unacceptable place; there were virtually no civilian inhabitants and little to damage. The objectives were purely military and tactical: control of the southern Mediterranean coast and the Suez canal, and the protection of oil fields. It was war in its purest form.

The desert sands were like an ocean; the ripples of the dunes vast, slow moving waves. The battle was as much with the topography as with the enemy. Roads were few, and short-cuts notoriously perilous. Rather then armies being able to spread out, they were channelled into corridors passable by lorries and tanks. The Allied troops adopted relatively conventional tactics, building up fortress-like strong points, but Rommel adopted a completely different tactic, preferring to amass his forces like a naval fleet, employing it like a vast Armada. Herford thought this was in fact a far more perceptive method of deploying forces in the desert, but it was not copied by the Allies, who owed their eventual success not to superior manoeuvring, but simply to the massive injection of American fire-power.

The work of the Motor Ambulance Convoy was vital, though

largely unglamorous, and only occasionally punctuated with moments of high drama. But even when the Convoy was ploughing to and from the scene of action to hospitals in Cairo, there was adventure of a different kind. Enemy movements were unpredictable, and it was not uncommon for solitary units to become isolated and even lost. Many roads which were safe earlier in a particular day were no longer safe by the evening. It was of vital importance that ambulances got through whatever the obstruction, so alternative routes had to be plotted and marked over the desert.

Herford soon acquired a reputation as an accomplished route marker. It required skill and accuracy with compass, aided at night by a knowledge of the position of the stars -something he had learned in boyhood. The ambulances carried tracks which could be unrolled in front of the wheels of a vehicle bogged down in soft sand, or caught in a depression or wadi, but the chief skill was in gauging the landscape and choosing a solid path. As Arctic explorers must learn to detect hidden crevasses, so desert navigators must avoid deep, soft sand and gullies. Both skills owe something to acquired knowledge, but a lot more to finely tuned instinct.

Another talent which also became invaluable was in scavenging vehicles left derelict by the enemy. Whether through lack of fuel, or being caught in a swift attack, both sides abandoned thousands of vehicles all over the desert. Sometimes the departing troops had time to destroy their transport before it fell into enemy hands, but more often than not lorries, even ambulances and tanks remained for the taking. The situation was ludicrous. Herford carried off a particular coup when he recovered a completely intact Italian ten-ton water carrier in July, which subsequently became a vital source of supply for his unit.

Martin Herford armed for the desert!

The desert war was unique in the degree of mobility enjoyed by the combatants. The main struggle was for domination of the coastal towns, the British having very few Mediterranean ports, but the battles were fought inland, and mostly by tanks, infantry playing a subordinate role. Thus, much of the warfare in the desert became known to the troops as 'horse stakes'. Allied tanks would pursue Germans into the desert for as long as supplies held out, but would then be forced to retreat at speed as the enemy regrouped, refuelled, and counter-attacked.

Unfortunately, it was a truism that until the appointment of General Montgomery in April 1942 as the Allied Commander in Chief in the desert, Rommel was the better leader. He was able to marshall his forces effectively and orchestrate them like a single entity – a masterly experiment at 'sea warfare on land'. He concentrated his exertions on one objective at a time, and even in retreat managed to maintain high standards of efficiency in re-grouping. Winston Churchill himself praised him as a splendid military gambler. In the

House of Commons in January 1942 he said of him, 'We have a very daring and skilful opponent against us, and may I say across the havoc of war, a great general.' It was also to Rommel's credit that in 1944 he took part in the conspiracy to displace Hitler, an adventure which would cost him his life.

The months of latitude in summer 1941 were a welcome period of acclimatisation and recoupment after the Greek maelstrom. Herford and his colleagues found time to take in the country, and even to swim in the Mediterranean. At Fuka, Herford was tempted by the sight of rocks one and a quarter miles offshore. He foolishly swam there and back without telling his companions. He returned three hours later, his friends having given him up for drowned!

On 3 August Herford received a bundle of letters and a postcard from Mary. They had not seen one another for eighteen months, but whenever the military postal system was properly functioning they corresponded as frequently as they could. Perhaps because he had spent two summers alone, or perhaps because he felt happier and more certain of himself in the desert, Herford cabled to her on 3 August, asking the simple question, 'WILL YOU MARRY?'.

Nearly three weeks later he had still not received Mary's reply when he travelled with a fellow officer, Peter Field, to Jerubub in a Blenheim aircraft on a visit to some outlying units combined with a trip to a Senussi Tomb. The short flight was uneventful, but on the descent the pilot mistook an unmade-up stretch of sand for the landing strip and shook the plane nearly to pieces hurtling over rough ground which tossed the aircraft back in the air, only for it to bump and shudder to an erratic halt narrowly avoiding complete disaster. They were more than a little reluctant to reboard the aircraft on the return leg, but fortunately they arrived back at base without further incident and still intact.

The reply came in a letter of 27 August. Mary agreed, but

suggested it would be better if rather than decide on a marriage date, they announce their engagement first. He replied the next day asking her to buy a ring and go ahead with the announcement. The military post wouldn't accommodate parcels, however small, so Mary had to venture out alone and buy her own engagement ring!

Full scale hostilities did not break out until November. General Auchinleck, who had replaced Wavell as Commander in Chief of the armies of the Middle East, had set his sights on the important Libyan port of Tobruk. Its strategic significance both as a port and as a route for supplies was such that it was one of the most valuable prizes in the desert. Rommel's forces were occupying it and the surrounding country 70 miles to the west.

On 18 November the Eighth Army, preceded by extensive aerial bombardment, drove forward, closing the ring on Tobruk from the south and east. A bitter three-week struggle engaging the might of the tanks on either side ensued. But in one critical place only infantry could be used. Some 20 miles to the south-east of Tobruk was Sidi Rezegh, a ridge about one hundred feet high, which, on its northern side was almost a cliff. From the summit it gave a commanding view of the desert to the south, as well as providing a natural line of defence. This ridge became the key to the relief of Tobruk.

On 4 December Herford's unit moved up to a camp known as Conference Cairn, just a few miles from the battle at Sidi Rezegh. The casualties were coming out thick and fast, many of them New Zealand infantrymen. On 6 December news came through that a number of wounded were lying up in a wadi behind enemy lines and needed pulling out. Major Johnston described Herford's response to this news in a letter he later wrote to Herford's father:

' . . . We were under orders to move soon to Tobruk, but things were very 'fluid' and I had no one to appeal to to find out the real state of affairs. Martin and Jim (a fellow officer) persuaded me to risk about one third of my entire unit in an endeavour to get those boys out. Had it succeeded all would have been well, but had it failed I'd have been out of a job. Well, we decided that it must be done and off they went through enemy held territory and got up there; when the drill was for Martin to go in and try and get the wounded out under the red Cross flag. That they got there a couple of hours after a column out of Tobruk had gone through is old history; but it showed the stuff he was made of. If he had pulled it off and had the luck to get there first it'd have been a DSO.

. . . This is not an unsolicited testimonial, Sir, but I think it is only fair that you should know he's first class and the greater the responsibility the better he does; only thing he can't stand and that's inactivity . . . He's impulsive and impatient; I used to think I was impatient but I have nothing on him.'

The next few days of battle were a flurry of activity, receiving the wounded, and dispatching the more seriously hurt to hospital in Egypt. Herford's duties also included reccies of areas which had recently been the scene of tank battles, both to look for wounded, and also to retrieve any serviceable vehicles. This was an unpleasant task, and involved poking through the charred and burnt out remnants of tanks, hoping not to encounter the grisly sight of blackened corpses inside the turrets. But they found many unburied corpses littering the battlefield, attracting obnoxious black swarms of flies. Sorting through the dead was the most gruesome task of war. Fortunately, the enemy suffered the majority of the casualties. At the conclusion of the battle the Germans and Italians had lost 33,000 men dead and taken prisoner. The Allies lost 2,908 killed, 7,339 wounded and 7,457 missing, a total of 17,704. But in loss of armour there was almost parity, with the Germans losing 300 tanks, and the Allies 278.

With the fall of Tobruk to the Allies, Rommel was in retreat, and his army was chased off to the south-west, several smaller towns falling to the Allies in their wake.

Herford entered the remnants of Tobruk on 16 December, but the ambulance convoy had to push on, keeping abreast of the German retreat. Several days later they travelled to the newly liberated town of Derna where his unit recovered 130 British prisoners of war who had been in a German military hospital.

The freed men were white and washed out, and suffering from the effects of malnutrition. But on the night of the 22nd they ate well for the first time in many weeks, feasting on the local produce which was richly abundant in this small town.

Christmas day was spent in a desert encampment. The ground was soft and muddy, the rain torrential, reducing many of the roads to quagmire. Herford's unit enjoyed a good meal in the evening with wine and beer, but were shaken to their senses by heavy German gunfire in the evening. The festivities were short lived. There were many casualties to be evacuated along the impossibly muddy tracks. New year's Eve was celebrated with six hours digging out a four-wheel drive three-toner stuck in the mud!

In spite of the deluge, clean drinking water was at a premium, especially for the ambulance units. And together with tins of petrol, cans of water were the most precious commodity. Over the next two weeks Herford spent a lot of time on the road, reconnoitring routes for the evacuation of ambulances, and liaising between field ambulance units. The journeys were often lengthy and sometimes unpredictable, so he made a point of insisting that his driver, Atkins, brought two Jerry cans of water with them when they departed in the morning. But Atkins was not blessed with a quick mind, and on several occasions forgot to bring the water. On one morning in mid-January Herford gave his driver a stiff reminder before they set out,

'For God's sake, Atkins, let's not have any more trouble with the water cans.'

They set off in a newly overhauled 15 cwt jeep, but without their knowledge, the vehicle had been incorrectly fitted with springs designed for the 30 cwt vans. While the road was still flat they proceeded without incident, but as soon as they hit a sizeable pot-hole which in normal circumstances would have presented no problem other than a slight bump, the jeep bounced off the ground and turned in the air. Fortunately Herford was thrown completely clear, and suffered no more than a minor crack in the scapula. But Atkins was caught in the overturned vehicle and his scalp was cut from left to right, creating a bloody flap of skin which hung down over his eyes. Miraculously he was still conscious, and when Herford made it back to the wreckage the first thing he heard was Atkins asking, 'Is the water can all right, sir?'

Fortunately Herford was able to hail a passing vehicle and get Atkins to the Sutherlands' No 2 Casualty Clearing Station where his face was stitched up the same evening, and confirmation received that he had done no more substantial damage.

On 23 January Herford learned that he had been promoted to the rank of Acting Major, and was posted as OC to the 16 Motor Ambulance Convoy. He felt that with only twelve months of service behind him, and given his almost complete ignorance of King's Regulations, the promotion was due in no small part to Johnny Johnston, who had recognised his 2nd I/C as a highly competent soldier.

The last week of January did not augur well for the British campaign. Rommel was regrouping to the south-west of the area around Tobruk and Benghazi which were newly captured by the Allies. However, unknown to the Allied commanders, due to British misfortunes at sea, the German army was being rapidly re-supplied via Tripoli. On 21 January Rommel sent three columns, each of approximately 1,000 motorised infantry to test the Allied defences. The columns succeeded in slipping through the gaps left by the front line infantry who were gathered together in strong points. This was an embarrassing gaffe for General Auchinleck. He had been caught napping, and now Rommel's forces drove forward with a sudden ferocity which necessitated a rapid retreat. On 23 January Auchinleck wrote confidently to Churchill in a telegram that,

'. . . it may well be that Rommel may be drawn on into a situation unfavourable to him . . . Am confident that General Ritchie is waiting for opportunity to force encounter battle in conditions which may be more favourable to us than those obtaining around Aghelia, with it's swamps and bogs and bad going.'

The next day the news was a little worse, Auchinleck was forced to concede in his daily communication that,

'. . . [Rommel's] initial advance seems to have disconcerted temporarily at any rate our forward troops . . . The situation has not developed quite as I should have liked, but I hope to turn it to our ultimate advantage.'

These shreds of hope were built on a total lack of appreciation of the extent to which the Germans had improved their supply lines. In the next few days they pushed forward with a vengeance, and re-took Benghazi, and much of the land to the south-east of Tobruk they had lost the previous year. It was an humiliating loss. Auchinleck tried hard to rationalise the defeat in his telegram to Churchill on 29 January:

'. . . It must be admitted that the enemy has succeeded

beyond his expectations and mine, and that his tactics have been skilful and bold . . . Rommel has taken considerable risks and so have we. So far he is justified by results, but General Ritchie and I are seeking every possible means to turn the tables on him . . . There is no disorganisation, or confusion, nor any loss of morale as far as I can see.'

The latter statement contrasted markedly with the situation on the ground. The British retreat had to be as rapid as the German advance. Roads were cluttered with hundreds of retreating vehicles fleeing from the enemy with little organisation or cohesion. Herford noted in one of the few brisk, diary entries he made, that the retreat was, 'Not impressive. Sloppy discipline and bad organisation.' Herford had himself to organise a night retreat of an ambulance convoy. This was an exercise which was normally avoided at all costs in the desert, due firstly to the dangers of straying off course, and secondly to the problems of vehicles loosing sight of one another in the darkness. The convoy was over one hundred vehicles long. Herford decided there was only one technique which would work, which was to travel at no more than a few miles an hour. This was the only way to ensure that the tail vehicles did not get left behind. Without the use of headlights he had to navigate by the moon and stars alone. At one stage the column was bombed, causing two casualties, but the next morning they arrived at their destination, Charruba, having only suffered two casualties.

The Allies held the line at Gazala and Tobruk, where they glared at each other until the end of May, neither side making a decisive move until Rommel again made a forward drive. Churchill cabled to Auchinleck that,

'I am reluctantly compelled to the conclusion that to meet German armoured forces with any reasonable hope of decisive success our armoured forces as at present equipped, organised and led, must have at least two to one superiority.'

In fact British forces were inferior to the German at that stage, and so began a frantic effort to pour weaponry into the Middle East in time for the major confrontation which was to take place later in the year.

The intervening months until May were a time of frenetic preparatory activity for the entire British army. Although there was no large scale confrontation, there was a constant background activity of aerial bombardment, and skirmishes at the ever fluctuating front lines. Herford's unit was kept busy constantly channelling in supplies to field ambulance units and removing casualties. Often these journeys were made over trackless desert where known locations were nothing more than a set of co-ordinates. These expeditions were a challenge in terms of navigation, but also a test of mettle in the sense that the risk of running into a German forward unit was constant. The desert was full of unknown quantities, and would not oblige at attempts to tame its ferocity.

In all these excursions, Herford had the reputation of a man with limitless energy who would constantly drive others on to match his stamina. But this relentless pace could not be maintained indefinitely, and in late February he suffered a rare bout of illness. Suddenly his temperature rose to 102°, he found himself sweating profusely and suffered acute abdominal and glandular pains. There was little treatment for these passing fevers other than bed rest, but time spent in inactivity, especially when accompanied by physical weakness, angered him considerably.

The usual pastimes for men in their precious leisure hours were listening to the radio for news of developments at home and the progress of the war elsewhere, and writing letters home. Every word written by servicemen had to be censored, so although Herford wrote countless letters, he wrote virtually nothing about his work or the progress of the campaign. Interestingly, he was not nervous of committing to paper his personal and transient thoughts, which, in the hands of a more repressive regime, might have been taken to count against him. In February 1942 his sister Sylvia wrote, and spoke generally of her agitation at the wartime bureaucracy, and her amazement at the fact that conscription of labour should have taken so long in coming. In philosophical mood, Herford replied:

> ' . . . Total conscription of labour should have been introduced long ago. All employed by the nation. The Russians must find us incomprehensibly indefinite and slip-shod. How will it work out afterwards? Will home affairs tend to run in the same grooves as after the last war? 'Anything for a footing anywhere' and a mad rush to make money, spend madly and enjoy recklessly. I hope there will be a very advanced degree of Socialism. British Communism. However, we shall each have our little worlds, homes and interests. Humanity is very stupid in the mass, but the world is still young . . . '.

Herford was not an overtly political man, and never became one. The hopes he expressed in this letter were not based on any political dogma, but an intense desire for the tools of organisation and good management to be brought to bear on the country as a whole. There was a feeling that the free for all in the 1930s had blinded politicians and public alike to the darker forces which were building up elsewhere in the world. There was an equal desire that the same mistakes would not be repeated once the war was over.

That the British troops in the desert were fully expecting victory is beyond doubt. Major Johnston wrote to Mr Herford Snr on 19 March 1942 that,

'We're all in great heart here, and I for one expect this war to be all over bar the cleaning up – and that will be a longish job – by late autumn of this year.'

Herford's letter to his parents of 15 March 1942 gives a more detailed insight into feelings at that moment:

' . . . Soon the hot weather will be here and then everything will dry up – till next year. Who, looking at the desert, would think that flowers were hidden? A little rain and the magic growth recurs.

Days pass quickly and there is quite a lot to do although there is a general quiet. Soon I hope for events and for a success which has merely been delayed. Taking into consideration the whole world position, I am very optimistic. I think there are excellent reasons for thinking that German morale and strength is on the ebb.

It is the shape of things to come after the war that bewilders me. It seems to me that then may be the time we shall reap the evils of war. The transition from a war organisation to a new order of normal life will be a fearsome business.'

A final comment made in a letter to his parents dated 22 May 1942 provides an insight of a different kind into the preoccupations of soldiers out of touch with developments at home:

'When we hear of the freedoms and equality which have been granted to women, one cannot help thinking that great things will develop in the future. I firmly believe that the future of humanity is largely in the hands of the women!'

The optimism displayed by Herford and Johnston in their letters of the earlier part of 1942 turned out to be a little misplaced. The next decisive moves were to be made by Rommel.

A strategic blunder by Generals Auchinleck and Ritchie led to the situation whereby the port of Tobruk was instated as a major supply port for the Allied forces, yet was not considered sufficiently important for proper defences to be installed to ensure its safety. The Allies' main priority was the defence of the Egyptian frontier, some 70 miles to the east, but Tobruk was a forward position, there was nothing of significance between it and the Egyptian border. Auchinleck did not want his army besieged in Tobruk, with the possibility that they would be destroyed and driven back into the sea.

Unbeknown to the British War Cabinet, Auchinleck gave orders in February 1942 that should they be forced to withdraw from Tobruk, ' . . . the place will be evacuated and the maximum amount of destruction carried out in it.' As a result of these orders the town's defences were allowed to dwindle. Mines were lifted for use elsewhere, anti-tank ditches silted up with drifting sand, and the wire perimeter fences were breached in many places for vehicles to pass in and out. The South African General Klopper, commanding the 2nd South African Division, was placed in charge of the town with ninety days' supplies. In total about 35,000 men were in occupation.

In the second week in June Rommel went vigorously on the offensive, driving the Allies eastwards. Herford's 16 MAC moved back 20 miles in intense heat in which every metal object became unbearable to touch. There was a heavy air of pessimism as they were pushed further back towards Egypt. They had not been led to expect that the enemy had sufficient morale and resources to inflict this level of damage.

Tobruk was swiftly surrounded by Rommel's tanks and pounded with heavy gunfire. To the south east all remaining British tanks were

128

thrown into battle at the road junction in the desert known as 'King's Cross', but the opposition was overwhelming them. Only a handful of tanks escaped and all British batteries were overrun. The Germans simply swamped the Allied forces with superior firepower. There was no realistic prospect of a relief column penetrating through to Tobruk for some days.

General Klopper was in a cleft stick. If he continued to resist he would lose many men, but if he tried to break out of the besieged town he would lose many more, due to an acute shortage of transport. Auchinleck urged him to keep on fighting, but on 21 June at dawn, to the amazement of many of his own officers, he offered the Germans his surrender, and 33,000 Allied troops were taken prisoner.

The news of the fall of Tobruk was deeply galling to Herford and his colleagues. On the morning of the 20th a Kitty-Hawk pilot landed near their unit and told them the news. He had been ordered to reconnoitre the area still held by Klopper for a landing strip, but had aborted when he received a message that the surrender had been made. The next morning a jeep containing eight soldiers and a sergeant arrived. They looked exhausted and dejected. Herford asked the sergeant what had happened. He was almost incoherent with anger and frustration. 'Tobruk's fallen,' he said, 'and that South African in command gave an order that none of the vehicles were to be destroyed, but our Brigadier said, "To hell with this" and told us to break up into small groups and see how many of us could escape. Nobody put up a fight. We were just ordered to surrender.'

The impression gained by Herford and others in the theatre of operations was that the South African troops and their leader were of doubtful loyalty. Many were Boers who still harboured a long-standing grudge against the British, and didn't see why they should perish for their old Imperial enemy. There seems no other credible explanation for why Klopper allowed so many provisions and equipment to fall undestroyed into German hands. Rommel's Chief of Staff recorded that:

> 'The booty was gigantic. It consisted of supplies for 30,000 men for three months and more than 10,000 cubic metres of petrol. Without this booty adequate rations and clothing for the armoured divisions would not have been possible in the coming months. Stores arriving by sea had only on one occasion – in April 1942 – been enough to supply the army for one whole month.'

The fall of Tobruk was seen as a Godsend by Hitler, who immediately wrote to Mussolini:

> 'Destiny has offered us a chance which will never occur twice in the same theatre of war . . . The English Eighth Army has been practically destroyed. In Tobruk the port installations are almost intact. You now possess, Duce, an auxiliary base whose significance is all the greater because the English themselves have built from there a railway leading almost into Egypt . . . The Goddess of Battles visits warrior only once. He who does not grasp her at such a moment never reaches her again.'

Following the fall of Tobruk, Rommel was immediately able to push on towards the Egyptian frontier without having to wait for supplies to be transported 1,500 miles from the west. For the remaining days of June and the early days of July the British were in disarray. Herford's unit fell back to the Alamein line inside Egypt, but the retreat was in chaos, not aided by the need to detect gaps in minefields laid to repel German tanks and heavy strafing from German plane.

Martin Herford with officers of 16 MAC, 1942. Herford is pictured smoking his pipe.

Once 16 MAC was installed in its new camp, Herford had to return westwards to oversee the continuing evacuation of casualties. On the night of the 3 July he was asked to reconnoitre an evacuation route through the Quattara depression, but soon became hopelessly bogged down in the loose sand, and it took many hours and exhaustive effort to rescue his jeep with the patient use of sand tracks. By the time he was making the return trip over 200 casualties were being evacuated by this route, and many lorries became marooned. The evacuation was becoming a disaster. Herford forged another path across the desert to the south which was eventually followed, but the casualties were transported to safety more by good fortune than good planning.

In mid-July Churchill paid a visit to the United States where he made an urgent plea for armaments, and was in the most part successful. Meanwhile the British took what advantage they could of the fact that Rommel had come so far so quickly, and launched a number of counter-attacks from the Alamein line. The battle swayed backwards and forwards until the end of the month, by which time both sides had fought themselves to a halt.

On the afternoon of 23 July, Herford was driving across the desert en route to visit the New Zealand and 2 MAC when he drove over a recently laid German mine eight miles south of El Alamein. The car was badly damaged, but he was visited by good fortune, and escaped with fragments of shrapnel in both legs and knees and a perforated left ear drum. He was patched up, splinted and sent to hospital in Cairo. The day after his accident he wrote to his parents telling them that he hoped only to be out of the fray for a few days, but it was to be November before he was well enough to return to his unit. The shrapnel wounds themselves were not serious, but he was physically exhausted, and they became septic. By 3 August he was discharged to convalescence, but a week later ran a temperature of 103 and suffered swollen glands. He was re-admitted to hospital, and it was 9 September before he was well enough to get out of his bed.

The timing of his accident could not have been more frustrating. Herford was fully aware that a major Allied offensive was planned, but it became increasingly clear that he would not be playing any part in it. In August, Auchinleck was replaced by General Montgomery, and a massive re-arming of the Eighth Army with American hardware took place. On 18 September Herford returned to the RAMC HQ, but Brigadier MacFie insisted that he should not return to the desert. He was convinced that Herford was battle weary and not yet physically strong enough to cope with months of little sleep and hard physical labour. Instead he was posted to No 15 (Scottish) general Hospital, where he remained until November.

The last week of October saw the battle of Alamein. The Allies had increased their armoury so that they now outnumbered the Germans two to one in firepower. The German line, approximately 15 miles to the west of Alamein, ran 40 miles to the south and was heavily fortified with minefields and anti-tank trenches. Hitherto they were adequately supplied, but several German oil tankers were destroyed in the Mediterranean causing a severe shortage of petrol. The German generals had little idea of the magnitude of the attack being prepared against them, and when it began on 23 October they were taken almost completely by surprise.

When battle commenced, Rommel was in hospital in Germany and his position had been taken by General Stumme. But within twenty-four hours of the start of the battle Stumme had died of a heart attack, and Hitler personally ordered Rommel to leave his sick bed and resume his command. This he did, but his forces were no match for the massed Allied guns. Like Napoleon, Montgomery went by the maxim that 'cannons kill men'. He launched relentless bombardments on key German positions, all of which had been accurately pin-pointed thanks to the de-coding of German secret messages transmitted using the Enigma machine. Rommel was in an unenviable position. Due to lack of fuel he could not hope to organise a successful retreat across the desert without being annihilated, but meanwhile he was suffering massive losses under Allied fire. He had no choice but to stand and fight. But after twelve days of heavy fighting the Germans and their Italian allies broke loose and went into full scale retreat (though the Germans gave themselves priority in transport and left many thousands of Italians in the desert with little food or water to be picked up by Allied patrols). At the conclusion of the battle, four German divisions and eight Italian divisions had ceased to exist as fighting formations. Thirty thousand prisoners were taken together with countless items of transport and rations. Churchill described the victory at Alamein as 'the hinge of fate . . . Before Alamein we never had a victory. After Alamein we never had a defeat.'

Herford's task after the battle was again to tour the battlefield and clear up the carnage which remained. In the town of El Alamein itself the flies were so thick in the air that they blackened the doors of houses. They blackened everything. He recorded that he could never have imagined that there existed so many flies in the world.

In the early months of 1943 Herford became increasingly frustrated at the relative inactivity of his existence providing medical services for an army in the Western Desert which was no longer fighting. After the defeat of Rommel at Alamein, the focus of attention switched to Tunisia, where operation 'Torch', the first Anglo-American landings of the war was underway. By May 1943 North Africa belonged to the Allies, but Herford was keen to get back to the forefront of the action. In April he was moved to No 200 Field Ambulance, which involved further sorties into the desert, but the Commanding Officer of the unit, Robby Robinson was almost fresh out from his War Office job in Whitehall, and had very little idea about the desert. Herford was therefore greatly relieved when he learned they were to be part of the invasion force going to Sicily. His unit left North Africa on 4 July 1943.

CHAPTER 7

SICILY

Herford set sail for Sicily in more confident mood than two years previously when he had been part of the ill-fated Greek expedition. Bolstered by the Americans, and with the Germans in increasing difficulty, he was fully confident that this expedition would be a successful one. The 200 Field Ambulance was attached to the 231 (Malta) Brigade as an independent group. They would share the same supplies, but their commands would be separate. Herford was grateful for this, desiring as much autonomy as he could obtain.

The expedition to Sicily was the precursor to the Italian invasion and the beginning of the battle for the continent of Europe. In mid-1943 the bulk of the German forces were concentrated on the Russian front, and although amongst the Allies Russia had the most powerful artillery and infantry, Churchill and General Eisenhower decided that efforts should be concentrated into diverting some of the German forces away from the Russian front to enable the Russians finally to overcome their attackers. Italy was the obvious choice for an invasion as Allied troops could be moved relatively swiftly across the Mediterranean from North Africa, and Sicily was to be used for a dry run to measure the level of resistance which might be met with on the mainland.

Operation 'Husky', as the Sicilian invasion was named, involved 3,000 ships and landing craft carrying nearly 160,000 men, 14,000 vehicles, 600 tanks and 1,800 guns; an immense logistical undertaking from which many lessons were learned in the invasion of Normandy.

The Germans knew that invasion was coming, but were short both on men and morale. On 20 May Hitler had a conference at which his Foreign Secretary, Neurath, reported that the Sicilian citizens were openly cursing German soldiers in the streets. They were blamed for causing the war and exhausting food supplies. The public officials were unwilling to exert discipline and the general view was that the arrival of the English would be a liberation. Increasingly Mussolini's power was being eroded by internal dissent. The Allies were hopeful not only that the Italian populace would welcome them, but also that invasion would provoke a popular uprising against their leaders.

The convoy arrived in the Gulf of Noto, south of Siracusa, at nearly midnight on Saturday 10 July 1943. The sky was shining red with phosphorous flares which were being sent up by the Germans twenty-five at a time. Any cover which the darkness afforded was effectively destroyed, but there was very little fire coming at them, only a few shells exploding harmlessly into the sea. The landing site had been well chosen as there appeared to be very little resistance.

Herford's unit landed at Marzamemi, 40 kilometres south of Siracusa on the bottom south-east corner of the island. The landings started at half past midnight and continued until dawn. The troops filed into landing craft which swept swiftly across the calm sea to the beaches where they quickly dug in – a precautionary measure, as the Germans were already in full flight having been subjected to heavy fire from the Allied landing further up the coast.

Herford's unit landed at 7 a.m. The sun was up and the German fire seemed to have dried up completely. He had anticipated being pinned down in hastily dug slit trenches whilst battle raged, but instead he had time to admire the glorious countryside – filled with rich green vines and tomato plants laden with ripening fruit, while the heavy transport was being brought ashore. A casualty centre was quickly erected, but there were few wounded; most of the injuries were limited to superficial wounds caused by stray shrapnel from the sporadic shelling offered by the meagre German defences.

By the time the unit's six ambulances and four three-ton lorries were brought ashore it was 10 a.m. Herford decided the best course was to reconnoitre a site for the casualty centre further inland. He set off with a driver through the gently undulating countryside until they found an ideal spot a mile inland in some well equipped farm buildings which bore signs of having been recently evacuated by German officers. The accommodation it would afford the limited casualties would be very comfortable.

A number of medical units besides Herford's had come over in the expeditionary force and were spreading out along the coast. Herford established his site as the central casualty station and during the rest of the day made a tour of the other ambulance units to ensure that their evacuation procedures were correctly in place. The Germans were digging in on the hillsides further inland, and any battle fought uphill would inevitably bring heavy casualties.

When Herford returned to the newly established base he received an order to constitute an Advance Dressing Station (ADS), to accompany a special composite heavy-striking force codenamed 'Harpoon'. The ADS would be in the front line of infantry picking up the wounded as they fell. It was the most hazardous of medical work, but he was extremely eager to be in the forefront of the action, and determined that medical services would be provided as close to the fighting troops as possible.

The order required immediate action, and he quickly prepared a three-ton lorry loaded with supplies and two light ambulances. The mini-convoy set off at once for Harpoon Force HQ at Noto, a small town some twenty kilometres to the north and five kilometres inland from the coast, arriving at 5.30 a.m. the following morning. There Herford reported to the CO, Brigadier Richards, and two hours later moved off in the rear of the Harpoon Force convoy.

The procession of tanks, heavy artillery and infantrymen struck inland in a north-westerly direction towards the small town of Palazzolio. Along the way there were frequent stops while small pockets of resistance were mopped up with barrages of artillery fire. But nearing Palazzolio the opposition became stiffer. Air support was called up, and British bombers remorselessly strafed the German strong points with dramatic effect. By 4 o'clock in the afternoon British tanks were rolling into the centre of Palazzolio and prisoners were being rounded up at rifle point.

Until the town was entered the Harpoon force had suffered no casualties, but as the remaining Germans were flushed out of their hiding places two British soldiers were shot, – thankfully not fatally. Herford's unit scooped them up, and he sent an ambulance back to the hospital at Noto with the British casualties and two wounded German POWs lying side by side.

Having gathered momentum, Brigadier Richards did not want to allow the enemy time to regroup, so immediately pushed on inland towards the town of Vizzini. They were now in potentially troublesome mountain country, but the Germans seemed largely to have fled. Herford could barely believe the speed with which they had penetrated the interior of the island. But hopes of a trouble free occupation of Vizzini were shattered when three miles outside town they met with extremely heavy, and very accurate mortar fire.

For several hours they were pinned down while the superior British artillery gradually wore the town's defenders into a slow submission. Meanwhile, Herford got word over the radio that another Advanced Dressing Station positioned on the outskirts of the town of Bucchari (which was several miles further back along the Palazzolio road), had just received five British casulaties as a result of an attack by tanks. The brunt was borne by the 7th Medium Regiment Royal Artillery, which received heavy losses of life. Herford responded by despatching an ambulance, which collected a severely wounded Private who had lost a lot of blood from a deep bullet wound. Frantic attempts were made to prevent the bleeding; a dressing was pressed hard against the wound and a saline drip connected to prevent the blood vessels collapsing, but tragically the life simply drained out of him during the journey.

Nightfall arrived and Vizzini was still in German hands. The dogged resistance continued into the next morning, when to everyone's surprise the mortar fire increased. Very little advance was made, and Herford was frustratingly holed up in the back of his ambulance. For a doctor to be at the front with very few casualties to attend to was an ironic experience, rendering him for the time being little more than a spectator, but he was grateful that for now at least, lives were not being squandered.

Under covering mortar fire two companies of the Hampshire Regiment attempted to make the breakthrough, but each time they were forced back by the ferocity of fire. The enemy continued to hold out for the rest of the day, taking advantage of the fact that so long as they remained in a town filled with innocent civilians, the ferocity of the Allied bombardment would be tempered by a concern not to inflict too much on the Sicilians.

That evening Harpoon Force was bolstered by the arrival of the 231 Brigade, bringing with it a welcome increase in firepower. In anticipation of a major assault being launched which might involve hand to hand fighting, Herford was required to set off with an ambulance to Vizzini to prepare for the arrival of the expected casualties. En route he stopped to help extricate Brigadier Urquhart's jeep from a ditch!

By the following morning the enemy had been beaten back from the town, their retreat necessitated by a shortage of ammunition. The Harpoon Force then divided in two. The objective was the town of Scordia. One half of the Force would go via Militello, the other via Francofonte. Herford's unit moved with the half going via Francofonte. There was slight opposition, but good progress was

139

made the following day and by 5 p.m. Herford had established 'A' Advance Dressing Station one mile east of Scordia.

The Allied campaign made steady progress northwards across the island, but not as swiftly as they would have hoped. On the East side the Eighth Army were struggling though mountainous country towards the port of Catania, and on the West, the Seventh Army were heading for Palermo on the northern coast. Although the Axis troops were initially taken by surprise, they did not take long to adopt strong positions, usually at altitude. The mountain roads were narrow, winding and often treacherous. The defending army frequently blasted cliffs above the roads making them impassable except by infantry. In hand to hand combat the Allies were in a much weaker position – there were 405,000 German and Italian troops on the island, outnumbering the Allies by 2½ to one.

The Harpoon force was now fighting across the plain to the south west of Catania and meeting stiff opposition and very accurate mortar fire. Herford was kept busy removing casualties to safety, but was dogged by a lorry breakdown on the night of 17 July which took the REME until 6 a.m. to repair. This was particularly galling as moving casualties at night was much safer than risking attention from enemy fighters during the daylight hours.

On the afternoon of 19 July, Herford received orders to join the other Advance Dressing Station which had been established at Raddusa, a small town to the north-east. Under cover of darkness the small ambulance convoy set off at 1 a.m., only to discover several miles to the north that the bridge on the Raddusa road had been blown. They were forced to take a diversion, only to get lost when in the pitch dark, without the help of headlights, the Raddusa road was completely missed. A circuitous route was adopted, more than once impeded by blown bridges, until they reached their final destination at midday on the 20th.

Raddusa was comfortably behind Allied lines, but Herford needed to visit the forward ambulance units to ensure the supply and evacuation lines were operating effectively. On the morning of 21 July he set off by trusty motorcycle to visit the C section of the Dorsets several miles to the north. All was well with casualty evacuation, but the enemy shelling was intense. On leaving Herford had a lucky escape; he unwittingly left his motorcycle in full view of the Germans, allowing a mortar unit to size up the range with considerable accuracy ready for when he came back to drive it away. As he started the engine several mortars in succession landed far too close for comfort, spraying him and the motorcycle with a stinging shower of earth and gravel. He counted himself extremely lucky not to have been among the 31,000 Allied soldiers killed and wounded in the campaign.

The following day he continued his liaison duties, visiting the 4th Canadian Ambulance Unit and the Devons, helping the latter evacuate their casualties south. As well as coping with the disconcerting accuracy of German fire, Herford also had to contend with an unexpected enemy when the farmhouse in which he was lodging turned out to be infested with fleas whose constant biting and hopping kept him awake most of the night.

On the 24th the Advance Dressing Station at Raddusa suffered a direct hit from a shell wounding seven personnel, one of them fatally. Those who remained unhurt considered themselves very fortunate. It had been yet another close call. Herford began to question whether his luck was running out, as the following evening, whilst he was in a forward position visiting the Devons, he was bedding down to snatch a few hours' sleep in a farmhouse when he heard the menacing whine of an approaching mortar. He held his breath, waiting for the worst; but, missing him by no more than a few feet, the motor crashed into the next bedroom killing the occupant. Herford emerged from the damaged building shaken but unhurt!

The following day he again found himself in the teeth of danger when he went forward with ambulance units to evacuate casualties from a wooded area to the south of Agira which was being doggedly defended. At one point he was standing at the top of a small hill held by Canadian infantry. Suddenly he heard a shout to hit the deck. German soldiers in camouflage rushed up the hillside staging a counter-attack. Weaponless, Herford could only watch as the Canadian infantrymen held their positions and opened fire on successive waves of troops who alternately leap-frogged one another, the men on the ground providing covering fire for those surging forwards. Bullets whistled overhead; the air was suddenly thick with the acrid smell of exploded gunpowder as spent cases sprayed from the breaches of the Canadian guns; and ears were deafened by a barrage of thunderous rifle cracks. Herford was in awe of the infantrymen as they coolly held their ground while at any moment they might find themselves in a battle of bayonets. But thankfully the uphill struggle proved too tall an order, and German fire suddenly ceased. None of the Canadians was hurt, but on the slopes below several twisted, lifeless bodies lay motionless in the scanty cover. At intervals, small groups of survivors sprang up and ran for their lives to the valley below. But they need not have feared being shot in the back, and in accordance with the strange chivalry of war, the fleeing attackers, though easy targets, were allowed to escape.

After the attack came the business of clearing the casualties. A number of Allied soldiers were lying injured in the surrounding woods and were rapidly fetched out by stretcher bearers. One of the greatest dangers to a soldier suffering a bullet or shrapnel wound is loss of blood, and the immediacy of medical attention was of critical importance. The field ambulances were equipped with limited facilities for carrying out blood transfusions – a recent innovation – which on this occasion saved several lives.

Herford's skill as a route-finder was called upon that evening when he was asked to find a northerly route which would by-pass the town of Agira, so tenaciously defended by the Germans. Herford was asked to survey some pretty rough and rocky terrain which proved quite impracticable for substantial troop movements. Apart from facing the lurking fear that wandering around in the darkness he would chance upon some enemy troops, he also had to sacrifice a night's sleep. He finally crawled beneath the covers at 5.30 a.m. and managed to snatch a few minutes' rest.

Fighting intensified throughout the day. An alternative northwards route had been found and the Devons and Dorsets made slow progress along a rough track to the east of Agira against stiff opposition. Herford followed, overseeing the removal of casualties, which were by now mounting significantly, but given the amount of metal flying through the air were still remarkably light. Again accurate mortar fire took its toll and four trucks suffered direct hits as well as the OC Devon's jeep. The OC survived, but two were killed and several others severely wounded. At the end of the afternoon the Dorsets took over a large house two miles to the east of Agira. Inside were two British soldiers who had been taken prisoner two days earlier and a German officer who despite swift medical attention subsequently died from his wounds.

The siege of Agira lasted through the night. The Devons and Dorsets with the help of Canadian reinforcements laid siege and showered in heavy fire from dusk till dawn when finally the weary occupants surrendered. With the town now occupied the quickest route back to the Advance Dressing Station was through Agira. Herford set off on his motorcycle but was stopped by a road block. He took a diversion over rough ground but struck a large stone and was thrown from his vehicle, the front forks severely bent. Reduced to shanks's pony he made his way on foot into Agira's outskirts where he found an old Italian car which he quickly cranked into life and used to return to the Advance Dressing Station.

The next objective was the town of Regalbuto, some ten kilometres to the west along a winding hilly road. Herford needed to move the Advance Dressing Station nearer the front line and decided that the house outside Agira in which the British POWs had been found would be an eminently suitable base. The Advance Dressing Station was quickly packed and moved forward. On the road north they had an alarming moment when a German soldier suddenly leaped out from a ditch at the side of the road, but fortunately all he wanted was to surrender.

For the next three days Herford and his unit were kept perpetually busy dealing with mounting casualties from the bitter struggle to enter Regalbuto. The occupying German and Italian troops put up tremendous resistance in what was in effect a final stand. There were divisions of Allied troops making rapid northwards progress along a wide front, and unless a serious hole was blown in the Allied front, the German commanders knew that complete retreat from Sicily was inevitable.

Regalbuto was bombarded savagely. The enemy responded with all they had causing severe casualties. On 29 July the ADS evacuated 51 casualties, on the 30th 69 and on the following day 111. In addition to the exchange of artillery, there was also close quarters engagement between infantrymen in the narrow rocky ravines around the town. This terrain was also hazardous for stretcher bearers, who were almost sitting targets as they picked their way across the stony ground to retrieve immobile casualties and then carefully pick their way back up the hillsides. According to the rules of combat medical orderlies were not to be fired at, but when the air was thick with indiscriminate fire the rules, even if obeyed, could not be relied upon.

The night of 1 August saw the final crumbling of resistance and the fall of Regalbuto. Herford retired wearily to bed, thankful that the carnage was in abeyance, but was kept awake half the night by some noisy mules mating in an adjacent field!

Herford spent most of the day searching for wounded among the debris and smoking ruins of Regalbuto. The ancient market town had been smashed to pieces. The buildings where only days before life had carried on as normal were empty shells, many completely demolished, others half standing, threatening imminent collapse. During his searches he chanced upon a garage, still upright, which contained a functioning Fiat car which he immediately requisitioned for ferrying his medical staff to and from the ADS.

The next day, just when the staff of the ADS thought the casualties from Regalbuto had been cleared, the town was suddenly plunged into chaos when it was bombed and machine-gunned by American planes, who had obviously not realised that it had been liberated! Thankfully their aim was very poor and no one was killed, but there were six serious casualties. As if one incident of 'friendly fire' wasn't gross enough, the following day the Americans mistakenly bombed a forward detachment of the Dorsets, causing one further casualty. These incidents underlined the unavoidable fact that with such a massive force comprising regiments from completely different armies, breakdowns in communications were not only inevitable, but their consequences could be dire. Given the relatively primitive nature of radio technology and the rugged terrain which frequently interfered with signals, it was extremely fortunate that so few incidents such as these occurred.

Throughout Sicily the Allies had been gaining the upper hand and the Germans were in rapid retreat. The campaign would be completely finished by 17 August with the evacuation of the last German soldier to the Italian mainland. The capture of Regalbuto signalled the end of hostilities for Herford's unit. The ADS dealt with residual casualties, and then on seven August moved seven miles to the east with a detachment of the Hampshires and took as their base a baronial hall owned by Baron Spitallieri Alessi. It was in a dusty and unused state, but after a swift clean-up operation it made a luxurious temporary base. Herford recorded in his diary that he spent an entire day in an armchair delighting in idleness and reading Vigny Cinq-Mere and a number of good French books. A rare indulgence!

On 9 August he was again on the move, catching up with the rapidly advancing front line. He passed through the village of Adana, skirting around the foothills of Mount Etna and finally arrived at the newly captured town of Bronte. He was temporarily held up on the road by shelling, but arrived safely in Bronte to take control of 25 British prisoners who had been under the care of Dr Veronica Giacinto of Palmero. Most of them were paratroopers who had been there nearly a month. They were dropped inland at the start of the invasion to hold strategic points whilst the main landing forces pushed inland. Progress had been considerably slower than anticipated and many had either perished or been captured. Whilst Herford was at the small hospital in Bronte they suffered a further wave of shelling, with several explosions occurring very close by. He recorded in his diary that the Italians worked remarkably steadily under fire.

Herford returned to the ADS with the grateful ex-POWs to find that a troop carrier had driven over a mine killing four and injuring several others. Often during a lull men became careless, forgetting the omnipresent risks posed by mines and snipers. No soldier could afford to relax fully even for a moment.

The final days of the campaign were a time of unaccustomed relaxation. There was even sufficient time for 231 Brigade to organise a gymkhana! The ADS unit moved a little further north each day, and on 15 August took over the villa of Baron Vicenzina Voces, another lucky find. There were only limited casualties to deal with, as enemy attention was now firmly focused on evacuating the island. On 17 August fighting officially ceased when the Allies entered Messina on the far north-eastern tip of the island, which had served as the embarkation point for the German and Italian troops fleeing to the boot of Italy. Herford and his men spent their time carefully checking their supplies and equipment, in full knowledge of the fact that they would shortly be pressing on into the mainland, where they expected even stiffer resistance.

During the intervening days before the Italian invasion a Brigade party with Tarantella dancers was a great success, and Herford took the opportunity to set off on an expedition up Mount Etna with his colleague Captain Paul. At over 10,000 feet, and over twice the height of Ben Nevis, it was a fair climb to the summit, but the effort was rewarded with spectacular views of the volcanic craters. That evening Herford wrote to his parents for the first time since his arrival in Sicily, painting a picture of a landscape surprisingly unscarred by war:

'Hot sun and everywhere richly cultivated soil. Long terraces of heavy-burdened vines rising to the hill tops and filling the valleys. Apples, pears and luscious figs. But chiefly grapes, hot sun-enchanted clusters with soft purple bloom. A lovely land and friendly people . . . the loveliest views I have ever seen and night scented jasmine at the head of my bed.'

Before the commencement of the Italian invasion on 3 September the major medical problem among the men was an outbreak of malaria, a disease now more or less absent from the Mediterranean countries. The treatment was quinine, primitive but effective: sufferers were accorded relief, but once bitten by a malaria-carrying mosquito the disease resides in the blood and can flare up unexpectedly at any time. It was essential that rapid measures were taken to prevent any debilitation in the men, already battle weary, most of whom would find themselves fighting through the Italian and the Normandy campaigns without respite. The struggle for Sicily had been relatively brief, but was costly in lives. The enemy reportedly lost 167,000 men from active service, 37,000 of whom were Germans. The Allies lost 31,158 killed, wounded and missing.

For his efforts in Sicily Captain Herford was recommended for promotion, and on 18 November 1943 was awarded the Military Cross. The *London Gazette* carried this glowing citation:

'This Officer was in command of the ADS working with units of the Brigade Group. Although his duties did not compel him to do so, this officer during the Sicilian Campaign was constantly amongst the forward troops tending to the wounded.

At Agira on 28 and 19 July, and again at Regalbuto on 1 August, the work carried out by this officer, at times under heavy fire, was magnificent. His presence acted like a tonic to the men and the prompt treatment accorded by him to the wounded must have saved many lives.'

CHAPTER 8

ITALY

On 26 July 1943, amidst great political dissatisfaction in Italy with Mussolini's leadership, the Italian King ordered Marshal Badolglio to form a new Cabinet, ending the Duce's 21 years in office. Two days later, despite assurances from the King that he would be looked after, Mussolini was interned on the island of Ponza. It was an ignominious end to the career of a fanatical leader whose delusions of Imperial grandeur had strained Italy's weakening resources to breaking point. Increasingly isolated through Hitler's reluctance to spare valuable troops to defend Italian soil, Mussolini had lost the confidence of the Italian people and then of the Grand Council of the Fascist party, which on 24th July voted by nineteen votes to seven in favour of a resolution calling upon the Crown to assume more power and for the King to emerge from obscurity. Following Mussolini's rapid demise Hitler became fearful of an imminent armistice between the new Badolglio government and the Allies. He laid plans to rescue Mussolini, to occupy Rome and to seize the Italian fleet. Italy, which had been neglected by the Germans, suddenly became its Achilles' heel.

Overtures were indeed made by the Italians towards the Allies, initially by the Counsellor to the Italian Legation in Lisbon, the Marquis D'Ayeta on 3 August 1943. He explained that the King and Badolglio wanted peace, but felt obliged to keep up a pretence of fighting in order to avoid a full blown German coup d'etat. Eisenhower despatched General Bedell Smith, and Churchill General Strong to open negotiations in Lisbon. Talks began on 19 August and continued in earnest until the end of the month. The Allies demanded

149

unconditional surrender but the Italians were fearful of massive German reprisals if surrender was announced before a successful Allied invasion of their country. The Italian government was particularly concerned that the Allies should land north of Rome and ensure the Germans were driven far north of the capital.

Finally on 3 September 1943, the day on which the Allied invasion commenced, General Catellano signed the terms of the surrender in Sicily. The Armistice was announced on 8 September, but Italy was still occupied by Germans and became the scene of some of the most bitter fighting of the war.

On 3 September Herford learned that he was to be part of a landing which would take place at the tiny village of Porto Venere two miles south of the port of Pizzo, which was 80 miles north of the main landings at Reggio, the major town on the far south-western tip of the boot of Italy. At 8 a.m. on 5 September his unit travelled along roads crowded with military traffic to the Sicilian port of Messina where they embarked on a small vessel bound for Italy. The views of the straits of Messina were dramatic, but a keen wind whipped up, making the launching of landing barges impracticable. It was therefore decided to postpone the landing until the next day, and the ship took shelter for the night in the harbour at Faro on the north-eastern tip of Sicily. Most of the men, including Herford, had to sleep on deck, so US army blankets were issued to all those huddling on the cold boards which kept out most of a sudden cloudburst in the night!

The next day the seas were still too rough to make the crossing. There was a dangerous sense of anti-climax and maintaining morale became a considerable challenge. The Senior Officers therefore organised practice landings to keep minds focused, but there was no disguising the fact that everyone was feeling tense and impatient. The crossing to Italy was finally made on the evening of 7 September. The wind had dropped, the sea was calm and the air warm. Herford fell asleep on deck, blissfully unsuspecting of what was to follow on the Italian beaches.

At 1 a.m. they arrived off what they thought was Porto Venere, but the skipper, who confessed that his knowledge of this part of the Italian coast was nil and his briefings sketchy, was unsure of their exact location. The situation was made worse by the absence of the expected marker lights which should have been positioned by the advance party. In fact there were no lights of any kind to be seen. The Captain cruised up and down the darkened coast for two hours before finally landing on a beach on which a tiny flickering red light had appeared.

The landing was effected without incident and there appeared to be no enemy presence in the immediate area. The first person they encountered on the beach was a rather bewildered private carrying the Brigade mail bag. Such was the level of disorganisation that there was no proper liaison with the advance party, and Herford stumbled around in the darkness trying to make contact with friendly troops. But as light dawned they were met by the OC and a Medical Dressing Station was quickly established in one of the buildings on the hillside overlooking the bay, not far from a railway tunnel with a single track line.

It transpired that Herford's unit had been unexpected arrivals, and as dawn arrived it was clear from a quick observation of the local topography that they had been extremely fortunate to land in the right place. Porto Venere was a tiny village perched on a hillside above the sea. The buildings were few, interspersed with small copses and scattered along ancient rocky terraces sloping down to the sea.

The peaceful scene was shattered shortly after first light with the commencement of brisk continuous gunfire from nearby enemy emplacements, followed by the arrival of German aircraft pounding the landing area with bombs. Further waves of troops landed throughout the day, but their arrival had been anticipated. The Germans seemed to spring from nowhere. Later in the morning at a spot on the beach immediately beneath the Medical Dressing Station, a landing craft off-loading men and equipment into the shallow water came under heavy fire from a gun close to the shore to the left of the beach. But despite the flurry of bullets rattling into the sand, the work of unloading continued steadily as if it were no more than a training exercise.

Throughout the day the intensity of fire increased as machine guns opened up from inland and mortars sang overhead. Supreme efforts were made to get men and equipment ashore as swiftly as possible, but inevitably in such an exposed position, casualties were high and there was a constant stream of injured to the dressing station. In mid-afternoon a further wave of bombers swept overhead discharging their lethal payload into the sand, which was thrown up in great heaps half burying several men who had to be dug out. Work continued frantically in the dressing station, treating casualties as fast as possible – stanching blood, cleaning wounds and applying temporary dressings. There was no time to share in the fear of the men still struggling across the beach.

As the minutes passed pressure on the Brigade perimeter intensified. The Hampshires put in a titanic effort in their sector, but despite their best endeavours some ground was lost. Shelling on the beach became still heavier. A landing craft received several direct hits, killing and wounding many. For a time the situation looked grave, and the thought crossed the minds of many of the men ashore that they would either be driven into the sea or slaughtered on the beaches.

Herford could see that the direct hits on the landing craft had created more casualties than the stretcher-bearers could contend with. They urgently needed help, so he ran down to the beach and waded waist deep into the water to the landing barge, which was by now almost empty save for several casualties. He waited with them, head ducked down beneath the steel sides of the vessel for the arrival of a stretcher party. When at last the stretchers arrived the injured were loaded as swiftly as possible, but they were one short. Herford assured the Private left behind they would be back and that he was safer with the benefit of the limited cover of the barge than being carried across an open area.

Herford then scrambled across the beach in search of other casualties, but fortunately found none. The stretcher bearers had done astonishingly efficient work. He began to pick his way back and had made it almost to the dressing station when a bomb dropped from a German aircraft exploded very close by. He dived down beneath a wrecked stone wall next to a sapper officer as large chunks of heavy debris thumped into the ground around them from repeated blasts. The brim of the sapper's tin hat was digging into the side of Herford's head, and in his frightened stupor, he found himself fingering the edge of it, at the back of his mind the thought that it might give him some cover.

After what seemed an eternity the raid ended. The two men tentatively picked themselves up and dusted each other down. Herford said, 'I think that's the last for this time.' The comment seemed fatuous, but the scene was wholly incongruous: a beautiful, clear sea, a sudden calm, almost silence, where minutes before all had been chaos. The stunning contrasts of war in such picturesque surroundings were almost too great to comprehend.

Herford returned to the dressing station and was relieved to see that the Private he had left to be collected from the landing craft was safely inside, but was not in grateful mood. As soon as he saw Herford he said, 'You're the bloke who left me behind.' Another man on a stretcher came to Herford's defence, saying to his fellow casualty, 'Well you beat him here by half an hour!'

Work was proceeding apace to tend to the waiting wounded

when shelling resumed and an ambulance outside the dressing station received a direct hit causing several fatalities. It was rapidly decided that their position was far too vulnerable and that the only safe place was the railway tunnel, even though there were almost certainly Germans at the other end. The medical personnel were all-hands-on in moving the stretcher cases into the shelter of the mouth of the tunnel. As bodies and equipment were hastily transferred, orderlies set about reconstructing a dressing station in the tunnel. They faced the obvious problem that at any moment the Germans could decide to fire into their midst from the other end of the tunnel, but in the dire circumstances it was a risk worth running.

The dressing station remained safe, though overworked for the remainder of the day. By nightfall there were about 300 casualties and the prospects looked gloomy as yet further wounded were brought in. A squad of sappers was sent up to recce the tunnel with a view to demolishing the other end to prevent it being used for a surprise attack, but they concluded that the demolition would be too dangerous.

By now it was becoming evident to even the most optimistic that the Brigade was making no headway in the face of fierce opposition and was in increasing danger of becoming irretrievably boxed in.

The situation suddenly underwent a dramatic transformation. News was received over the radio that Italy had announced her unconditional surrender. Then contact was made with the 5th British Infantry Division which had successfully pushed up the coast ahead of their Brigade and was now in a position to reinforce them. Finally they heard that the American invasion force had made a successful landing at Salerno. As the fighting stopped everyone cheered.

The announcement of this armistice brought an almost immediate cessation of hostilities from the enemy, who were obviously forced to withdraw at once. No one doubted that the

Germans would continue to fight on as an army of occupation, but for all practical intents and purposes their objective thereafter became to hold the line from just south of Rome to the northern borders, a task which they accomplished with some success and at considerable cost in lives over for the rest of the year and into 1944.

At 4 a.m. on 9 September Herford helped load 154 casualties who urgently required evacuating onto a landing craft beached close to the entrance to the railway tunnel. The enemy fire had fallen ominously silent, and despite the flurry of activity on the beach not a single shot was fired. There was an almost ghostly hush. The Germans had hastily withdrawn inland to regroup further north destroying roads and bridges as they went

The following morning was a perfect, warm autumn day. The bright sun rose in a clear sky and reflected on the azure sea. The gentle waves lapped almost noiselessly on the sandy shoreline which the day before had been the scene of so much slaughter. In place of the dreadful whine and crash of mortars was the soothing sound of birdsong. Where did the birds shelter when chaos descended? Herford wondered, and marvelled at the resilience of nature, which even in the thick of war never seemed to be defeated.

For his part in the landings at Porto Venere Captain Herford MBE, MC was awarded the bar to the Military Cross. The Citation in the *London Gazette* of 13 January 1944 reads:

'On the 8 September 1943 during the assault on Porto Venere (Italy) an LST (landing craft) which had been shelled during the approach and set on fire arrived on the beach. Major Herford led a stretcher party to the beach and assisted in the rescue and evacuation of casualties from this LST which was still under well aimed shell fire from a flank.

This officer dressed several casualties which occurred in the LST during which time it was also dive bombed. Throughout this period the officer carried out his duties calmly and without regard for his personal safety. By his coolness, leadership and courage he was the means of saving many lives.'

Herford subsequently commented that the eulogistic terms of this citation were 'unrecognisable exaggeration', but there could be no doubt that his actions in retrieving casualties from the landing craft exposed him to mortal danger. A danger which, no doubt, his businesslike, efficiency allowed him largely to discount once he had made his decision to cross the beach. But he would also be the first to acknowledge that there were many feats of astonishing bravery that day from all the men who worked tirelessly to unload their landing crafts in the direct line of enemy fire.

Herford's unit spent the next ten days moving swiftly northwards with the Allied troops chasing the retreating Germans up the heel of Italy. By the 19th they had arrived along infinitely twisting roads at Lagonegro, a village 666 metres high at the base of Mount Sirino. Heavy artillery pounded away at enemy positions all night, but it was nonetheless a beautiful spot. The Germans had blown a vital bridge which was seriously holding up the Allied advance. Time and again in the coming months this would be their tactic, destroying vital communications in their wake rather than standing their ground.

As the Allies advanced from the South and the Americans pushed inland from Salerno, the affairs of the Italian government took further unexpected turns. As the Germans closed in a tight circle around Rome the King and government removed themselves to the southern town of Brindisi where they attempted unsuccessfully to exercise authority over a people for the time being plunged into chaos.

Attempts were made to co-ordinate the groups of Italian partisans who now turned their weapons and ingenuity against the Germans, but these were largely self-organising outfits and the writ of the Badolglio government ran not much further than the city of Brindisi.

Lieutenant Colonel Martin Herford, Antwerp 1944.

Mussolini had meanwhile been moved from Ponza to the island of La Maddalena off the coast of Sardinia; then, fearing German interference, Badolglio had him moved to a small mountain resort high in the Abruzzi in central Italy. But on the morning of 12 September 1943 90 German paratroopers were dropped by glider near to the hotel where Mussolini was being held. They effected his removal and carried him away in a light aircraft to a meeting with Hitler in Munich. Having secured assurances of extensive German help, the Duce then returned to establish a rival government in the north based on the shores of Lake Garda, which he maintained with varying success until his ignominious execution at the hands of Italian partisans in April 1945.

Herford's brief spell in Italy drew to a rapid close as on 22 September his unit was returned to Sicily. At first they were given to understand that they were being posted to India, but then received the gladdening news that they were returning to Britain. They left mainland Italy on 23 September and spent a pleasant but frustrating four weeks waiting to embark on the *Tameroa* bound for home. The eight day journey via Algiers, past Gibraltar and through the bay of Biscay passed largely without incident until they were nearly home. In the Irish sea their escort vessel flushed out a submarine with depth charges and then opened fire with deck guns. When the vessel surfaced it was discovered to be British!

On 5 November Herford stepped ashore at Avonmouth and with the rest of his unit left almost immediately on a train bound for Sudbury in Suffolk, where they arrived in heavy rain at 5 a.m. and marched to camp. The sudden exposure to the cold and damp had given him a heavy cold and bronchitis. He was exhausted but it was good to be back.

He had been away from English soil for three years and nine months.

CHAPTER 9

1944 – A TOUCH OF PROVIDENCE

To be back in peaceful England was a tremendous relief. Despite the ravages of war it still looked clean, collected, cheerful and purposeful. Herford's first thoughts on arrival were of Mary, his fiancée whom he hadn't seen for nearly four years. He immediately telephoned her and five days later met her at the station where they had an emotional reunion.

Their thoughts turned swiftly to marriage. Herford knew that sometime in the new year the Allies would launch the long awaited invasion on mainland Europe. It was inevitable that his unit would be involved and that he would be away from home for some considerable time (they didn't expect it to be the 18 months it became!). So they decided to seize the opportunity while they had it and quickly made arrangements for the ceremony to take place on 15 December at St John's, Clifton in Bristol, where Mary was working at the children's hospital.

Their wedding took place early in the morning, followed by a reception at the Royal Hotel. They left at 1 o'clock and drove to the north Devon coast for a brief honeymoon in the Lynmouth Hotel. The weather was bracing, strong winds and rain, but they fearlessly braved the elements taking long walks and drying their steaming clothes in front of a log fire. They had waited four years to be together, and the English winter weather was not going to stop them enjoying their few precious moment before Martin rejoined his unit.

On 29 January 1944 the Director of Medical Services, Colonel Tomlinson, told Herford that he would be given command of a field ambulance unit and asked if he would like one in the Airborne Division. Herford expressed an open mind on the subject and so a week later was summoned to an interview with Colonel Austin Eagger who was Director of Medical Services of the 1st Airborne Division. He was not particularly impressed with the applicant from the RAMC and asked 'Why do you want to join the Airborne? I've got more than enough willing and competent officers I would like to promote. Do you actually know anything about the Airborne?' Herford confessed that his knowledge was limited to his experiences in the RAMC. Eager pulled a face. 'Do you know what "stick" morale is?' Herford didn't. Eagger ended the brief interview with the offer of a position of second-in-command of a field ambulance. Herford considered this for only a few seconds before replying emphatically that he would prefer to make his way to France by boat as he had done before in Sicily and Italy. He left with the distinct impression that Eagger had no intention of letting an upstart land-lubber permeate the ranks of the elite Airborne Division!

Herford was comforted to read some years later that a contemporary of his, later to become Major General Urquhart, had experience considerable difficulty when he arrived from outside to take over the command of the 1st Airborne Division. He wrote, 'On January 7th 1944 I drove to Fulbeck to take over the Division. I was received with some surprise and a good deal of curiosity, and I was soon to learn that an Airborne Division is a rather self-contained community, into which one had to be accepted . . . I was aware of being looked over closely and with ill-concealed reservations in some quarters. I had plenty to overcome. To make the situation rather more complicated, one of the brigadiers had been given to understand unofficially that he would be in command.' Herford did not regret having been warned off by Eagger, but as events were to later unfold on the continent, he would have plenty of contact with Airborne officers at Arnhem.

The first three months of 1944 passed with a tedium and sense of purposelessness only the military could devise. Herford was greatly relieved to escape the confines of rural Suffolk in mid-March when he was transferred from Sudbury to the invasion concentration area in Brockenhurst in the New Forest. At that time the entire south of England was slowly gearing up to launch the greatest invasion in military history – Operation Overlord.

The Brigade to which Herford was attached, the 231, had spent six years in the Middle East, including three especially hard ones in Malta, which had come under intense aerial bombardment. The soldiers were tired and quickly grew impatient of being confined to leaky bell tents in the New Forest with no floor boards, no recreation and perpetual rain. Security was intense for fear of German spies so everyone was confined to camp. Needless to say, this was too much for many of the men to bear, and large numbers of them disappeared for hours at a time 'absent without leave'. Being an officer Herford had no choice but to make the best use of his time he could, but was usually holed up in his tent with a book. The highlight of the wait in the New Forest was a visit by General Eisenhower who carried out an inspection. Herford's impressions of him were favourable, but he was far from awed. He wrote to his parents that 'The men liked him. I thought he appeared an able and humane man. A good leader, not necessarily brilliant but able to get men to work and combine well.' He might have been commenting on a Corporal!

The draft plans for 231 Brigade's part in the Normandy operations were examined in detail and briefings held Herford was then posted to 163 Field Ambulance in Hampstead, his new command. He was greatly relieved to be freed from the claustrophobic tents to comfortable billets on the edge of London.

He found the 163 Field Ambulance Unit efficient and in high morale. His only complaint was that they had been trained in a technique called the 'New Formation Method', designed to maximise the number of casualties attended to on the battlefield by treating them where they lay, then moving on to the next, leaving the job of removing them to back-up staff. This concept horrified Herford, who could not abide the idea of a wounded man lying outside without shelter, wounds dressed or not. He sent his Quarter Master out with several men to scavenge for some large tarpaulins in the local dumps, insisting that if casualties were to be treated on the field they should at least be gathered together and sheltered in make-shift tents. This hybrid technique was later employed with good effect at Arnhem.

Herford's unit embarked at Southend for France on 18 July 1944, nearly six weeks after the initial D-Day landings. Operating as an independent unit, they followed the Guards Armoured Division through the low country of Belgium and Holland to the Rhine near Arnhem. Progress was swift and steady. The American heavy artillery and troops at the fore drove forward to the Rhine, where the Germans dug in and put up solid resistance. Herford was fortunate throughout August to be operating largely behind friendly lines, busy organising the evacuation of casualties, which were thankfully comparatively light. This was a time of hope and optimism, the Allied progress seemed unstoppable, and the faces of the cheering crowds who lined the streets of the towns and villages along the route were sufficient reward for all the years of hardship and suffering endured by the men who had now become their liberators.

The situation in Belgium was confused as German troops were in hasty retreat, often leaving their positions without warning. On the morning of 4 September, the day after the liberation of Brussels, Herford set off with a fellow officer, Captain Franklin, to reconnoitre the area around Malines with a view to establishing a Corps Medical

Area in the vacinity. Taking the main Ninove-Brussels road, they crossed the Canal de Charleroi and turned north towards Vilvoorde which they reached an hour later. They were instantly struck by the fact that there were no flags out and the streets were almost eerily quiet. The few people who had ventured out looked at them with surprise and even suspicion. When Herford stopped and asked one of the nervous locals whether there were still enemy soldiers in the area they were told that they had left only hours before. Within minutes a small crowd of people had gathered around the staff car – these were the first Allied soldiers they had seen! Some were overcome with joy, but others seemed to doubt whether they were British at all. When Herford assured them they were, the Belgians said they had not expected to see Allied troops for some time, and assumed that when they did it would be Americans.

Rather rashly, Herford decided to continue along the Malines road, which was the route by which the Germans had evacuated. They soon reached the next village, Eppeghem, where they were told that the Germans had left no more than one hour before. Herford ordered his driver on, but proceeded slowly, making careful inquiries from the civilians they passed at the roadside. One woman they stopped was extremely frightened, thinking she was being tricked by Nazi agents, but when she realised they were British she broke down and wept for joy. A little further on they reached the village of Sempst where they were told that there were still German troops only a short distance ahead.

They crawled along the road, speaking to everyone they encountered, and then met a small group of ragged looking civilians who said they had been internees in a German POW camp and had just released themselves following their captors' flight. But they warned that there were still Germans sheltering in a house a kilometre along the road.

Herford decided to investigate. He ordered his driver to proceed to the house, suspecting that the only reason German soldiers would not be in full retreat would be because they were desirous of surrendering to the British. Even at this early stage the more realistic amongst the German soldiery were confronting the fact that surrender to the Russians would be no guarantee of fair treatment in accordance with the Geneva convention. Fortunately this assessment proved to be correct. As the staff car approached the house three German soldiers emerged with their hands on their heads and surrendered. Herford seized their weapons (being medical officers they were unarmed) and ordered them to remain where they were until British troops arrived. They looked miserable and obviously had no stomach for further fighting. It must have been a great relief to know that for them the war was over.

As Herford was disarming them an excited group of civilians ran over with the news that there were still some enemy troops in a nearby château, and insisted that they go there straight away. Herford ordered the car to the château entrance, which was a 100 yards back down the road to Sempst, but found that the large iron gates to the driveway were chained and padlocked. He thought better of single-handedly taking on a flushing-out operation, but assured the locals that more troops would be arriving shortly.

He decided to proceed a little further along the road to Malines but as he returned to the car the three German soldiers who had surrendered rushed along the road and asked if they could be taken with them back to base. Herford replied that there was simply no room. He left them at the roadside happily eating apples and talking to some civilians with little revenge!

Proceeding along the long straight road to Malines they crossed the bridge of La Senne and approached a junction with a side road. Just as they were coming onto a junction another car slowly turned out in front of them containing three German NCOs. Herford ordered his driver to pull round in front of them, then leapt out into the road

164

and demanded their surrender. The NCOs were startled and looked at each other in amazement. They clearly had no intention of surrendering and thought they were still in a safe area. Herford had no idea whether or not they were armed, but strongly suspected that if weapons were drawn he would be the one who ended up as a prisoner! Thinking fast he exclaimed in German that there were British tanks surrounding them and that surrender was the only sensible course of action. They consulted each other briefly and peered up and down the road in some disbelief. Herford bolstered his bluff by saying that they had better hurry up if they preferred to remain alive. The ruse worked. They reluctantly got out of their car and gave up their pistols. When Herford searched the car he found a large stash of weapons including a number of rifles, revolvers and hand grenades. There were also half a dozen bottles of first class brandy which he promptly requisitioned on behalf of the King!

Herford questioned his captives closely and discovered they were a party of demolition engineers who were very angry at having been captured in such an unexpected fashion. He ordered them to get back into their car and Captain Franklin, holding a loaded revolver, sat in the back with one of them. The two cars then set off in convoy along the road to Brussels. On the way between Sempst and Eppeghem they passed a party of German infantry at the roadside who seemed too surprised to interfere with their progress. Herford had effectively taken them behind enemy lines.

By the time they arrived back in Vilvoorde the streets were heaving with ecstatic crowds. Everywhere there were improvised flags and showers of flowers. The town had burst into life with people dancing in the square, embracing and drinking wine in a spontaneous outpouring of relief. As Herford's party drove through they were showered with petals, but some consternation was caused by the fact that the lead car contained Germans. It took them a few moments to realise that they had been taken prisoner.

Herford returned to Nledberg, his temporary base at that time, and deposited the prisoners. He still had to find a new site for the Corps Medical Area so he set off again an hour later. They had gone no more than a mile when they were stopped by a tank commander who assured them it was extremely unsafe to proceed further, as the canal bridge two kilometres ahead was mined and under fire from German 88 mm guns. It was the same bridge Herford and Franklin had crossed at 8 o'clock that morning! Satisfied there was no prospect of setting up a base in the Malines area they settled for a site bordering the main Brussels-Antwerp road where they moved later that afternoon.

Some days later Herford was informed that there was going to be a substantial airborne landing at Arnhem. Having reached the Rhine the Allies faced tougher and more resolute resistance which required bold counter measures. To cross they had to seize bridges which would carry military transport. Montgomery therefore planned to seize a bridgehead at Arnhem using the 1st Airborne Division later supported by the Polish Brigade. The 82nd US Division would be sent to capture the bridges at Nijmegen and Grave and the 101st US Division would secure the road from Grave to Eindhoven. The XXXth Corps would then push through from Eindhoven to Arnhem along the 'carpet' of airborne troops who would have seized these positions.

The operation was huge and hastily planned and involved 35,000 men. On 17 and 18 September many thousands of paratroopers were dropped. The 101st US Division was largely successful, but ran into problems when they discovered the canal bridge on the road to Eindhoven had been blown. However, they succeeded in capturing the town on the 18th. The 82nd US Division made headway, but could not seize the bridge at Nijmegen. At Arnhem some of the British paratroopers succeeded in holding their position at the northern end of the bridge over the Rhine, but were coming under increasingly savage attack. The XXXth Corps, which Herford's unit was following, proceeded up the Eindhoven road under heavy fire, frequently being forced to stop, but finally made it to Eindhoven on the afternoon of the 18th and the canal was bridged. The following day they pushed through to Nijmegen where on the 20th there was a hard fought battle for the bridge.

The final objective was to link up with the paratroopers at Arnhem, who were by now in dire straits. Bad weather had hampered the flying-in of supplies and ammunition was in short supply. The 10,000 men of the 1st Airborne gallantly held on to a small area on the northern bank where they fought for eight days, but the XXXth Corps, the 43rd Division and the Polish Parachute Brigade were all unable to reach them. All thoughts of a completely successful outcome to the operation were now abandoned, and the priority was to effect a 'rescue'.

Herford came up to the south bank of the Rhine on 23 September near Driel, 15 kilometres west of the town of Arnhem. As they had come closer the fighting had become more and more intense. The roads were clogged with military transport and further progress halted as the enemy held the vital bridges the Allies were struggling to capture. Herford met with Brigadier Eagger, the CO of the Airborne Forces medical services. He was dreadfully worried about the 1st Airborne pinned down on the opposite bank as they were reported to have nearly 2,000 casualties and were critically short of supplies.

Later that day Herford attended a conference of Senior Medical Officers at which it was decided that he should take command of the Airborne 'tail' of about 15 ambulances, including six vehicles with medical supplies for the Polish Brigade who were several kilometres further east on the south side of the river. With the assistance of Captain Louis of the 1st Airborne, he was given the task of seeing what could be done to get medical supplies over the river.

They set off in a convoy of seventy-eight vehicles. They had not gone far when Major General Thomas of the 43 Wessex Division flagged them down and yelled, 'What the hell is a medical unit doing here? I want guns!' He ordered them off the road to make way for heavy artillery.

Communications with the 1st Airborne had all but broken down. Units were separated, their locations uncertain, and no one knew exactly where their front line was, or indeed if they had managed to establish a front. They were surrounded by a ring of fire and were increasingly at the mercy of superior forces.

From the southern side of the river at Driel, Herford watched in amazement as supply drops were made on the other side of the river with awe inspiring bravery. Though the sky was an inferno of exploding shells and flak, the heavy, lumbering supply planes droned low over the ground and disgorged their pay loads of essential cargoes. The airmen inside could actually be seen throwing the bundles out of the doors. Planes were hit, they caught fire, spiralled out of control and exploded in the air, but the others carried on regardless. Herford describes the actions of those men as some of the bravest he witnessed in the war. All the more tragic that it later transpired that most of the drops had taken place over areas already recaptured from the Airborne. The Germans had apparently intercept the code signals for the drop and forced their way through so the supplies would come to them.

Of 100 bombers and 63 Dakotars on that mission, 97 were damaged and 13 shot down. Of 391 tons of supplies, only 31 were retrieved by the Airborne troops.

Herford waited in anticipation throughout the night of 23 September for an anticipated attempt to send reinforcements and supplies over the Rhine, but the mission was prevented by a lack of assault craft. The fire was so heavy on the roads that the necessary transport had simply been unable to get through.

On the morning of 24 September Herford had become increasingly impatient at their apparent inability to render any assistance to their helpless comrades on the opposite bank. He reviewed the alternative possible courses of action and later that morning sought an interview with General Thomas at 43 Division HQ. He found the General and put forward three options:

The first was to send two Medical Officers and 12 men in six DUKs (amphibious vehicles), each carrying half a ton of medical supplies from the Seaborne tail of the Airborne Division which could cross later that night. The second was for one officer and 30 medical orderlies, each carrying an assault pack of medical supplies, to cross in boats that night: and the third was for a daylight attempt to be made to carry over supplies in boats under the red Cross flag.

It was agreed that the last was potentially the safest, and would not rule out attempting either of the other methods if it were to fail. At 2.30 p.m., together with Captain Louis and four volunteers from 163 Field Ambulance (Privates H W Belmore, A H Hill, J J Keegan and A Moore), Herford organised a river crossing with 6 cwt of supplies. They were protected from enemy snipers in their position by the high banks of the dyke, so before they carried their supplies over the top and down to the water Herford asked the officer in charge of the platoon covering that section of river bank to provide them with covering fire if the Germans decided not to respect the Red Cross flag, but if they were forced to ground by enemy fire they should open up with whatever they had.

They made their way down to the river bank and were fortunate enough to find an assault boat which was to have been part of the aborted crossing the previous evening. No shots were fired and no Germans were visible on the opposite bank. The river was wide and fast flowing, there were high sloping grassy banks either side of it, rising 30 feet on the north side, levelling off, then rising steeply to some woods 200 to 300 yards away. The nature of the incline on the northern bank was such that anyone at water level could not have been seen from the woods, which was the most likely place for an enemy detachment to have taken cover. This was probably why this assault boat had escaped destruction.

Just as they were about to land on the other side another boat suddenly appeared from around a bend. There was only one man paddling and as he drew closer another figure rose up from the well of the boat. They had been part of a detachment who had attempted to cross the river the night before but which had been continuously pinned down by fire. Herford exchanged a few brief words, pointing them in the direction from which they had climbed over the dyke, then proceeded across the water under the Red Cross flag.

Unbeknown to Herford at the time, his party reached the north bank of the Rhine at almost the exact moment a truce ended between the Airborne and the Germans during which no fire was exchanged to allow for the wounded to be evacuated. The truce had lasted from 3 p.m. until 5 p.m. when the battle recommenced as if it had never ceased. History later revealed that at the time the truce was granted the Germans were becoming increasingly worried by long-range shelling from the British south of the Rhine. A message was received by Major Skalka (Chief Medical Officer 9th Panzer SS) from 2nd British Army HQ asking if the cease-fire could be extended to allow sufficient time for medical supplies to be brought across. Skalka refused.

Herford worked out that there were three possibilities. Enemy fire might terminate the proceedings forcing a rapid retreat; their luck might hold sufficiently for them to get through to the Airborne with the supplies; or direct contact would be made with the enemy in which case he would request safe passage under the Red Cross flag. The latter seemed the most likely possibility, so he decided to constitute himself an envoy and request an interview with a senior

German officer.

He surveyed the landscape. There was no movement in the woods ahead, but there was mortar fire issuing from a point under cover some distance to the right. It was impossible to say whether this was an Airborne or enemy position. Some 500 yards away to the left, situated on the edge of the woods, was a small house flying the Red Cross flag. There was a neat privet hedge around it and further up the hill behind it were several other houses. Between the river and the house was a line of willow trees.

Herford decided that the best option was to head towards the house. He left his party by the river and set off up the bank and a grassy incline beyond towards the willows. He saw the first signs of life just as he was approaching the willows. A group of soldiers emerged from one of the houses. From several hundred yards distance their nationality was not clear. Herford though it distinctly odd that they made no signal. He wondered whether they were Poles and prayed they were not Germans. As he drew closer he came upon a deep ditch filled with water, protected with barbed wire and difficult to cross. As he was looking up and down for the best place to jump over, a line of figures rose up from behind the privet hedge surrounding the first house; they pointed their rifles at him and made motions of throwing hand grenades. There could be no doubt that they were Germans.

The ditch was a nuisance. Herford had no desire to get wet and tangled up in barbed wire, but it was clear from the urgency of their signals that he had to hurry or they would open fire. He waved to them, raised his Red Cross flag, pointed to the ditch and walked along until he could find somewhere to cross. He marched up to them as boldly as he could and said, that he wanted to see *'ein hoher Offizier'* and asked to be taken to their Colonel. They asked whether he was a *Parliamentaire* (envoy), to which he replied that he was. It was apparent that the others still waiting by the river had no means of escaping, so he also asked if they could be brought with him.

The Germans were uncertain as to the status of this request, but no doubt Herford's persuasive manner and grasp of German were a distinct advantage. One of them took the Red Cross flag and said he would take him to their Officer. Herford spelt out that if they would not accept his status as an envoy the whole party should be respected and returned to the southern bank.

The Germans said very little apart from *'Ja, ja'*, and immediately blindfolded him. He was then led some distance on and told to stand against a tree. For a fleeting moment he wondered if he was simply going to be dispatched on the spot. The only grain of comfort he could summon up was the thought that if that was their intention they would have shot him as he was crossing the ditch. However, a few moments later a young soldier came and led him away by the hand up the hill over some rough ground. Walking blindfold was not easy, but the young German politely warned him of obstructions. After they had been walking for about five minutes Herford asked if they were near their destination. The German soldier had been shouting out questions to others he had met and it appeared that there were very few officers in the area. No one appeared to know where their HQ was.

The blindfolded walk continued for what seemed a long time, but was perhaps no more than half an hour. On several occasions there was mortaring nearby and Herford's escort seemed reluctant to go on; he pulled him down into cover once, but the shells exploded some distance away. In addition, a number of planes roared overhead firing their machine guns, but Herford concluded they were German planes strafing the Airborne.

Eventually they got to what Herford assumed was the battalion HQ. He was told to stand outside until an officer came out and spoke to him. Several minutes later Herford heard the voice of a young man who was evidently the officer who had been asked to deal with his request. Herford outlined his demands: the immediate passage of the supplies, the passage of further supplies, facilities for the immediate evacuation of the more seriously wounded Airborne troops and the return of himself and his companions should these demands be rejected.

The blindfold was then removed. Herford saw the officer was a young, good looking Lieutenant Colonel of an SS Group. His face bore a duelling scar, the mark of a young aristocrat. He requested Herford's identity papers and asked whether he had eaten. When Herford said that he had, the man seemed quite offended that he had refused the invitation to dine with them. He left and Herford remained standing outside looking at the guards and soldiers who passed. Some of them had hard brutal, war-worn faces. He felt distinctly uneasy about his safety.

Dusk was advancing and Herford was beginning to feel pangs of hunger. As he waited two girls of about twenty-two came out, evidently nurses, and they spoke in German. Herford learned that one of them came from Hamburg and had spent a year in Manchester before the war. When they mentioned food he reckoned that he would not get anything until the next day and so readily accepted. One of them fetched him a chair and a plateful of stew. As he was eating, a rather severe looking officer passed who thought that Herford was seeing to much, and told him to eat facing the wall. Through the open door Herford could see a tray of wine glasses being carried into the mess. He could hear the officers' voices and laughter as they exchanged jokes. It seemed a very civilised and relaxed mess.

A lady came out with a girl of eight. She was Dutch and explained that the house belonged to her. The Germans had just requisitioned it and had taken over every room except for one tiny one. Her daughter was forced to sleep on the kitchen floor. There was so much noise neither of them could rest. Herford sympathised.

173

The situation was comical, almost surreal – a woman complaining about the noise of laughter when all around them war was raging.

As darkness fell Herford's papers were returned to him and he was taken by car to the nearby Divisional HQ. He was now well and truly separated from the others in his party. He later learned that they had been allowed to return to the south bank, but that Captain Louis made a second attempt to cross later the same night during which he was shot and killed.

On arrival at Divisional HQ his papers were again taken for careful checking. Prior to the crossing he had taken pains to ensure he was carrying nothing other than his identity documents, some personal letters and a small notebook containing bogus 'top secret' information about some units which were well known to the Germans. He was pleased to see that they spent a considerable length of time poring over its contents.

He repeated his demands. The German officers stressed that the Airborne attack had all but collapsed and that they were unsure about his status as an envoy because he carried the Red Cross flag and not the white one. Herford replied that as he was a medical officer and solely interested in the wounded the Red Cross flag was sufficient.

This was not an argument they were prepared to accept. They agreed to treat him as a special prisoner and said that the next day he would be sent to see the Chief Regional Medical Officer, Lt Colonel Sangerling, who might be able to assist with the evacuation of the casualties.

Herford was then driven to another location near the town of Ede where he spent the night in some very uncomfortable accommodation: a cold room with no mattress and only one blanket. There was an armed guard posted outside his window. As he lay shivering in the darkness he admitted to himself that he had probably embarked on a fool's errand.

When Herford failed to return with his companions he was posted as 'missing, suspected POW'. As soon as the news reached his old friend Johnny Johnston, he wrote to Herford's parents giving his frank assessment of the situation:

> 'I have notified over 100 men as 'missing' in this war; they are just posted as missing for a very long time until official confirmation (of death) comes through. I therefore agree with you entirely about the War Office not saying 'believed POW' unless it's very sure of itself . . . Personally I've no doubt that he's safe and well although a POW. In fact I'm sure of it and frankly am not as worried about him as I would be if he was just 'missing'. And what's more it's nearly over now and it won't be long till he's restored to you again . . . That is of course, if he doesn't escape in the meantime, and I'd not put it past him! Bet he'll be a pain in the neck to any Germans he has to deal with officially . . . How proud you must be of him. You know, the magnificent Arnhem show was just his cup of tea. I know of no other friend who was so guaranteed to produce the goods under conditions like that as Martin. Here's hoping when he comes out that he has that DSO to pin up.'

Johnstons's remarks were prophetic in more than one sense.

Early on 25 September, Herford was taken to Schlöss Haetloo (Queen Willhelmina's Castle), a large German military hospital near the town of Apeldoorn in the Netherlands, where he was introduced to Colonel Sangerling. They met in the luxurious private apartments of the palace where they had coffee from some delicate china blue and gold cups.

Sangerling had a kindly demeanour and seemed to be treating Herford not as a prisoner but as one medical man to another. He carefully explained that the German hospitals in the Apeldoorn area had become overwhelmed with over 2,000 of their own wounded, and that he had just heard that over 1,500 British casualties were being evacuated from the battle area. In the normal course of events the Germans would have undertaken to have treated them, but they had completely exhausted their facilities. He expressed the fear that the wounded would simply have to be evacuated in cattle trucks; there was no alternative.

Herford repeated his request for passage for medical stores or evacuation over the river. As the Germans were obviously intent on carrying out their obligation to treat the British wounded it seemed foolish for them not to accept an offer which would be of logistical assistance. Sangerling seemed interested in the proposition and went away to make some phone calls.

By an ironical coincidence, at about the same time Herford was having this discussion with Sangerling, arrangements were being made for all survivors of the 1st Airborne Division to pass through 163 Field Ambulance following their retreat across the Rhine. Under unceasing bombardment the order had finally been given to evacuate. Many were shot trying to swim to safety across the river, many were captured. In total 1,400 Airborne troops were killed. Of the original force of 10,000 only 2,400 returned. The 163 Field Ambulance provided hot drinks and blankets for all returning Airborne personnel and treated the casualties promptly, providing shelter with the tarpaulins Major Herford had 'collected' and made into tents.

It soon became clear that Colonel Sangerling was not in a position to allow Herford to return, but he tried to find a way in which he could be used to help the stream of injured British paratroopers who were being brought into Apeldoorn. Sangerling began by taking Herford to view the Willhelm III barracks in Apeldoorn which he said he might make a post for 500 walking wounded. He was expecting many stretcher cases as well, but simply did not have the resources to provide for them.

Next Sangerling took Herford on a tour of the hospitals in the area to make clear to him the parlous nature of their situation. At one point Herford was left alone with Sangerling's driver, who came out with the strange comment that in the five years he had been working for the Colonel he had never been punished. Herford concluded that German officers were usually expected to mete out penalties to their staff!

During the tour of the hospitals Herford had the opportunity to talk to many of the British wounded, including a young doctor from the Airborne, Captain Theo Redman of 133 Field Ambulance, who had been wounded in the arm and captured on landing. He had thereafter worked with a German surgical team treating British and German casualties alike without distinction. He told Herford that a large number of Airborne medical staff had been captured, including two whole field ambulance and surgical teams who were now working at the St Elizabeth Hospital in Arnhem.

Herford quickly concluded that the Willhelm III barracks could be used as a hospital for the British wounded. He pointed out to Sangerling that the Allies were amassing in great numbers just over the Rhine and that it would only be a short while before Apeldoorn fell into enemy hands. It would therefore be better for the Germans to evacuate their casualties before the town was overrun and leave the Allied casualties to be collected by their own side. He even went so far as to suggest that he might be able to get petrol and supplies transported over the Rhine to help with the evacuation of German casualties.

Sangerling was not impressed with the idea of accepting help from the Allies, but was anxious to explore all the possibilities. Herford again pressed his request to form a hospital at the barracks and finally Sangerling gave in. However, he sought a personal assurance that the building would be used for no other purpose, saying, 'A hospital must be a hospital and nothing more.'

Herford collected Theo Redman and a few orderlies and proceeded to the barracks. By the afternoon casualties, mostly walking wounded, were pouring in. At that stage they had virtually no medical supplies, and Herford complained bitterly to Colonel Sangerling that arrangements should be made for some of the supplies captured from the Airborne to be made available. Sangerling himself didn't have authority to grant the request, but agreed to drive Herford to Arnhem to speak to (General Bittrich).

Sangerling and Herford travelled in a German staff car along the Arnhem road past streams of displaced Dutch, many of whom had been rendered homeless by 'friendly fire'. There were a number of RAF and USAF strafing planes in the area who could not help but injure some of the civilian population. It was a sad fact that when Dutch surgical teams from Amsterdam arrived in the area two days later their initial task was operating on members of the civilian population who had been injured fleeing from Arnhem. (Sangerling himself was reported killed in his car during an air attack several months later).

When they arrived at Arnhem Herford was again blindfolded and taken to General Bittrich's command post. After a brief discussion (during which bombs from Allied planes landed uncomfortably nearby), Bittrich decided that Herford had heard and seen too much to be considered anything other than a prisoner. He allowed the blindfold to be removed, and with a smile said he was a 'special prisoner.' Herford objected, perhaps a little too impertinently, that he resented being classified as a prisoner at all. Bittrich replied that he thought he would not want to return in any event, implying that his first duty lay with the injured men of the Airborne. Herford replied that he would be glad to stay as long as he remained useful.

Bittrich turned out to be a reasonable man. He said that Herford could go to St Elizabeth's Hospital in Arnhem to request for help to be sent to Arnhem. He said he would consider the request for the release of captured supplies a little longer.

With the benefit of this minor concession Herford and Sangerling went to St Elizabeth's Hospital and arranged for the transfer of supplies, but by the time they arrived back in Apeldoorn over 600 casualties had been brought to the Willhelm III barracks. Many were walking wounded, but among the stretcher cases there were some who were dying.

By nightfall still no help had come from Arnhem and over 800 casualties had been admitted. There was little more they could do than make them comfortable. Most of the wounded slept the sleep of utter exhaustion, having hardly slept since the beginning of their ill-fated expedition.

In the small hours of the morning a German doctor arrived and said that they were to prepare 500 walking wounded for immediate evacuation to Germany. Herford and Redman were forced to go round the building waking men who had not slept or eaten properly for several days, telling them that they were to be taken into Germany. They gathered without complaint and mustered as if on parade. Herford watched with pride as in the chill dawn they formed up and marched down the road singing. It was an inspiring sight.

Soon after a second order was received, this time to select 40 stretcher cases for removal in cattle trucks. Herford took a chance and refused point blank to move any of the stretcher cases he threatened that there would be hell to pay if he was contradicted. The Germans demurred, but no more was said.

The following morning it was discovered that supplies from Arnhem had in fact been brought by English personnel, but that the English Major, Peter Smith, together with two other officers and twenty orderlies, had been brought by the Germans from Arnhem and locked up for the night. None of them could speak German so the mistake was not rectified until they had spent a very uncomfortable night in custody. As the confusion was being sorted out, Sangerling arrived with the news that the Willhelm III barracks would henceforward be officially recognised as an Airborne Hospital, and that they were to have full control of the food and supplies which the Germans would provide from their own stores.

The formal recognition of an official British Hospital was an enormous breakthrough and completely without precedent in the whole course of the war. In the few weeks in which it existed it was responsible for saving the lives and limbs of many men who otherwise would have had to wait their turn in German military hospitals. It is undoubtedly a fact that although Herford has received no official recognition for this particular achievement, the existence of the Airborne Hospital at Apeldoorn was entirely due to his persuasive efforts with Colonel Sangerling.

For the rest of the day the barracks hospital continued to receive British casualties. Thankfully the next day they were joined by two complete Field Ambulances commanded by Lieutenant Colonel Arthur Marrable, CO of 181 Field Ambulance, and Lieutenant Colonel W C Alford CO of 133 Para Field Ambulance. Their arrival meant that Herford was free to spend his time cajoling and scavenging for medical equipment and supplies. The tight-knit Airborne community had also begun to demonstrate its advantages as the officers and men quickly formed efficient working parties based on their existing organisational structures.

The last to arrive was Colonel Graeme Warrack, Assistant Director of Medical Services 1st Airborne Division. Just before capture he had removed his badges of rank in the hope that he would be less likely to be immediately transferred to Germany to a Senior officers' POW camp if he masqueraded as a private. This strategy worked well for getting him as far as the hospital, but once there he wished to resume his authority and be recognised as an officer by the Germans. Warrack attempted to remonstrate with a German NCO who responded by threatening to march him off into custody for insubordination. He did not, at any time, wear badges of rank.

Thanks to Herford's intervention Warrack managed to establish his position, and, as the Senior Officer present, next morning called a conference of Senior Staff. Herford briefed them on what they had managed to achieve since the hospital had been established and the strategy they were attempting to adopt, i.e. making the wounded comfortable in anticipation of a rapid Allied advance while making all possible attempts to prevent evacuations of British wounded to Germany. Warrack was impressed with what he found and appointed Herford as his second in command. Herford felt this was a singular honour given the closeness of the Airborne to one another, but his abilities as a German speaker were doubtless a significant factor in his appointment.

The major problem they now faced was feeding nearly 2,000 men in the now overcrowded barracks. At first the only cooking facility was a horse drawn field kitchen which was adequate for feeding only 250. Meals were therefore meagre and wretched. Nothing was worse for morale than hunger. The local Dutch offered what they could: blankets, items of medical equipment and food parcels, including a box of smoked salmon. Herford and Major Simon were delegated to divide it up between severely wounded men. It was a tortuous task; both men were aching with hunger but couldn't eat a scrap.

Herford again approached the German officers and protested vehemently that they were not being allowed to use the main kitchens which would have been adequate to cook for all the men. Again the Germans acceded to his request, and with the benefit of Red Cross rations which arrived from Canada they were able to eat more comfortably.

Talk soon began among the officers of escape. Herford was approached by a Captain Coke who told him that he and several others had established contact with the Dutch underground and that everything was arranged for four of them to make their escape that night. Coke himself had a wounded thigh and had sent a message to the Dutch requesting them to make a signal with a flashlight if they felt unable to risk him coming with them with the burden of his injury. Four days later Colonel Sangerling told Herford that several British prisoners had escaped. He found it rather ironical, for if the British really were coming so quickly it seemed ludicrous to risk being killed escaping over enemy territory.

It transpired that the escapees Sangerling had referred to were another party, but several days later Coke did escape with several others. Following this escape, however, the Germans decided the hospital presented a risk to security and adopted a policy of evacuating as many British casualties to Germany as they could.

When the evacuations commenced Herford again risked incurring the wrath of German officers by demanding the wounded were provided with the best possible facilities, objecting absolutely to any suggestion that they should be transported in cattle trucks. The results were quite astonishing, and even prompted Colonel Warrack to describe it as 'pure Alice in Wonderland'. On one occasion the Germans provided a specially appointed ambulance train with medical staff and nurses – conditions which exceeded those the German wounded could expect!

The German strategy now seemed rather self-contradictory. Whilst taking Herford to visit several Dutch hospitals in the area to investigate the provision of further medical supplies, Sangerling expressed his concerns for the German casualties. As more and more German towns were being destroyed by Allied air raids the hospitals available to treat them became fewer and fewer. The situation had become so critical that German medical units were deliberately leaving their more serious casualties to be treated by the advancing Allies. This should have added strength to Herford's arm in arguing that the best option was for the British to be allowed to remain in Apeldoorn, but administrative decisions taken above Sangerling's head dictated otherwise. The Germans were perhaps gambling on the Allies not bombing hospitals inside Germany where British POWs were known to be patients.

On the morning of 30 September two German surgeons arrived at the Airborne Hospital and made a cursory inspection of the wards before pronouncing that nearly everyone there was 'transportable'. Herford took grave objection and argued that besides the fact that they would be better off evacuating their own wounded, the journey was far too arduous and the nights far too cold for many of the men to be moved in safety. When that failed to impress the stony faced German doctors he threatened to make an official complaint through the Red Cross.

The protests cut no ice. Later in the afternoon Sangerling arrived with the order that 300 lightly wounded were to be evacuated in a 'truck train' (goods wagons). Herford said that no casualties would be prepared for evacuation unless assurances were given that adequate minimum conditions would be provided. The best Sangerling could offer was the posting of a German MO to the hospital who would ensure good supplies to the remaining casualties and deal with requests.

Over the next two days Herford had the unfortunate task of seeing more than 500 men off in German trains. He managed to secure the important concession that the wagons were to have a red cross painted on the roof to discourage strafing, but was horrified when on arriving at the station he saw a massive anti-aircraft gun being used right next to the train, inviting attention from Allied bombers! He complained loudly to Sangerling, who apologised and promised that there would be no more firing while trains were in the station.

Herford drew some comfort from the fact that at last the Germans seemed to be on the defensive. As he travelled through the town to and from the station the Dutch openly gave the 'V' sign, much to the annoyance of the German guards. Discipline was also beginning to break down among the German troops. On one occasion Herford saw that they were confiscating all the bicycles in the town – now the most valuable loot they could lay their hands on!

The hospital had been arranged startlingly quickly, the administrative side being run by Lt Colonel Marrable and the medical wing by Lt Colonel Alford, under whom were highly efficient teams of doctors and orderlies. An inspection was carried out by senior German officers including General Mayer and General Haubenreiser, Director of Medical Services Western Area, who were impressed by what they saw, though loathe to admit it.

However, no sooner had an efficient hospital been set up than the German began to run it down by steadily carrying out more and more evacuations which, despite protests from Herford, he simply was unable to prevent.

CHAPTER 10

ESCAPE FROM APELDOORN

Herford had been a POW for two months. It seemed like years. Having enjoyed unimaginable success and co-operation from the Germans, he now noticed a sudden and hostile shift in their attitude. Their annoyance had some justification: Graham Warrack was encouraging escapees and there was relatively little fencing to prevent it.

On the night of 8 October a Dutch doctor was coming to the Airborne hospital bringing 800 books for the men. En route he was arrested and the books confiscated by the SS. Herford made complaints but they were ignored.

The following day a previously co-operative German guard made offensive remarks to a British orderly. When challenged by Herford he made no apology and merely threatened him with arrest. That evening 600 German troops arrived to occupy part of the barracks which had been evacuated.

The complete shift in attitude was made clear the next day when Sangerling's second in command, Major Krammer, arrived and said that British personnel would only be allowed to travel to other Dutch hospitals with an escort. Previously Theo Redman and Herford had enjoyed free association with the Dutch and had driven unaccompanied in ambulances. The Gestapo had taken objection to this.

The guards at the hospital trebled in number and tightened their grip. No one was allowed to speak to the Dutch in the absence of a German interpreter. Signs increased that it would not be long before the hospital would be closed down entirely and those remaining sent to Germany. The St Elizabeth Hospital suffered that fate and the British medical personal and a Chapalin, Dan McGowan, were relayed to Apeldoorn.

Warrack called a meeting of senior staff while they still had the freedom to talk to one another without Germans listening. A decision was made that any medical personnel who wanted to were free to escape. Warrack suggested that approaches be made to the Dutch underground, but Herford was against it. If a Dutchman was caught harbouring a POW it would almost certainly mean instant death, whereas the recaptured escapee stood a good chance of merely being taken back into custody. Reliance on the brave resistance workers meant putting their lives in jeopardy.

Herford suggested, to Warrack the top priority should be finding a hiding place within the hospital so that in the event of a sudden and unexpected evacuation they could conceal themselves. Warrack agreed and it was decided that a hide-out equipped with food and water would be set up.

Herford expressed his keenness to make an escape attempt quickly, and offered to take with him the extensive lists which had been made of the wounded who had passed through the hospital, as a message had been received through the Dutch resistance that the War Office was anxious for information on surviving POWs.

Herford bided his time. Until now he had neither felt the need nor had the time to plan the most efficient method of escape. Tension increased on the night of the 14th when the Quarter Master escaped, and on the following night three doctors and two orderlies. A curfew was imposed and a group of officers were caught studying the only 1:100,000 map they possessed of the Apeldoorn area.

On the night of the 16th Major Krammer arrived and said that they would all shortly be removed. The guard patrols were increased further. A roll call was held and Herford had the distinct feeling that they would be moved out the next day. His time was short.

Herford had no food supply for an escape attempt, but he did have an army issue compass 'reclaimed' from a German ambulance driver who had carelessly left it lying next to him on the driver's seat. He also had a large scale map of most of the route he wanted to follow to the Rhine, together with a small map of an area of the river which he had singled out as being the best place to cross. It was situated in an area called the Heelsum swamp and he anticipated this would be unfit for human habitation or for slit trenches, both of these requiring firmer ground.

He held in his mind a clear picture of the German soldiers he had run into after crossing the river. They were set well back from the river bank, far enough to be invisible to anyone at the shore. He felt certain that if he could find a similar location he would be at a great advantage for getting across.

His plans for escaping from the hospital were hazy. It occurred to him that he might arrange for a small group to go between blocks with a guard carrying a covered pressure lamp. They could stage an accident with the lamp and while the guard's vision was affected by the glare he could slip away into the darkness.

He told his idea to Warrack and Marrable who immediately replied that it was too risky, especially as the perimeter of the hospital grounds was likely to be crawling with guards who would instantly be alerted by such a trick. Marrable suggested it would be better to squeeze through the small window in the operating theatre on the ground floor. They were least likely to be disturbed in the operating theatre. It was a moonless night, windy and pelting with rain. Perfect conditions!

They went upstairs to the sparsely furnished room where most of the officers were sitting around chatting. When they heard that Herford was going, several others said they wanted to come too. Herford was surprised and pointed out that any more than two at a time would increase the risk of detection, but said he would be prepared to take one other.

Dan McGowan, the Roman Catholic padre from the St Elizabeth Hospital in Arnhem, was extremely keen to come. He had a fearless reputation. Herford had heard how he had done splendid work on the battlefield at Arnhem, and afterwards moved freely among the Germans identifying the dead and helping casualties. He had thought of an escape route through the woods at Oosterbeek and hoped to go with Sandy Flockart, a dental officer, who was not so enthusiastic.

Herford strongly expressed the view that woods provided obvious cover for slit trenches and German movement undercover, and that they should stick to the route through the swamp. Herford agreed to take McGowan. He assumed that as he had a clearer idea of exactly what he wanted to do McGowan would simply follow. They had no more than a few minutes to get to know one another. Seldom could two people more ignorant of each other's characters have set out together on an enterprise which would involve such a deep level of trust. In a letter Dan McGowan wrote to Herford on 22 September 1979 he recalled the swift pace of events that evening:

'You remember we, Sandy (Flockart) and I, were preparing to escape together. Then, Sandy said that he felt his place was with the men, and the next thing is he was asked, because of his size, to hoist me – and you first, I suppose – through the upper window of the operating room. It still does not explain why I escaped at all; why I switched partners, if I had the scruples of escaping at all as a chaplain and leaving the men who were also prisoners.'

Thankfully Dan had prepared a small parcel of emergency rations on which they could manage for a couple of days. They hoped they would be able to forage for the rest, or perhaps even pick up a loaf

188

of bread from a friendly local. Dan also had an escape compass. From the front it looked like an ordinary collar stud, but if the white paint was scraped off the button, a tiny compass was exposed.

Having hastily finalised their plans they went downstairs to the operating theatre and laid out the equipment for a fake operation in case they were interrupted. With Sandy Flockart's help they moved a heavy wooden table under the window with a chair on top and the window was propped open by means of a broom handle lashed to the opening louvre. The drop to the ground was some nine feet, but even though it was no great distance it was decided to lower themselves down with the assistance of two knotted blankets, half inside the window, firmly secured, and half outside.

When the preparations were complete they switched off the lights and stood in silence listening for any sound. They waited for several minutes but could hear nothing except the gusting wind and heavy rain pelting on the windows. Herford decided it was time to go.

The upper section of the window was small and took some squeezing through. As he was hauling himself out Herford had brief second thoughts as he wondered what he might be letting himself in for. He had taken an irreversible step.

On landing he waited in tense anticipation for Dan to force his bulkier frame through the narrow gap. He helped Dan to land, they hurried across the tarmac path at the edge of the window and lay flat on the grass beyond. His heart was beating so heavily he could barely catch his breath, let alone hear the footsteps of any guards. Dan followed, and due to his size made a rather inelegant landing. Herford made him lie down in the grass while he carried out a quick reconnoitre of the hospital grounds.

Herford moved through the darkness looking for the best route to the perimeter wire. The pitch black night proved a mixed blessing as he almost bumped into one sentry! Herford retreated to find Dan and suggested they try another direction. They crawled across the grass until they came to another path. They lay frozen as a guard strolled by, waving his flashlight to and fro. The beam seemed to pass right over their heads, but miraculously they had not been seen.

They darted over the path and crawled through a muddy potato patch on the other side. Herford suddenly heard the voices of two sentries near the wire. He listened intently for a few minutes as they walked up and down their stretch of the perimeter. When the guards reached the end of their beat he turned round to whisper to Dan that they should move on. Suddenly someone nearby moved: there was a third sentry he had not identified who was standing against a wall only yards away. For a heart stopping moment Herford thought he must have been seen; but the heavy rain was obscuring them. They edged slowly backwards. When they were far enough away not to be heard, Herford joked to Dan, 'There's just one thing we've forgotten – to tell the others to leave the window open so we can get back!'

Herford selected another point to approach the wire, and this time found no guards. The wire itself was only a single coil which presented no real obstacle and they were over in moments and out across the scrub land beyond. They looked back at the gleaming lights of the hospital – the blackout was very poor.

It was a little after 9 p.m. and they had until dawn to cover as much of the 25 miles to their crossing point as they could. Herford's plan was to travel south west across open country to the village of Otterlo about 13 miles away. From there they would turn south to the Rhine. Walking at night would depend chiefly on compass craft and a good deal of guesswork.

They walked for about an hour, through fields and scrub, until they came to what appeared in the darkness to be a road. This was a mystery as neither of them recalled the maps showing a road in this position. But when Herford went to cross he had an unpleasant

190

surprise when it turned out to be a dyke! The surface shining in the occasional shafts of moonlight had given it the appearance of shiny black tarmac. Dan quickly helped him out. Herford was chiefly thankful that he had taken the precaution of tying his compass on a cord around his neck, otherwise they would most likely have lost their most valuable escape tool!

They continued in single file. This allowed Herford (who was leading) to listen for suspicious noises, and minimise the risk of their both being surprised. The negative aspect was that they occasionally lost touch and Herford had to retrace his steps to find Dan.

The tricks of light continued. A short while later they came upon what they thought was a dyke, and followed it for a short distance before realising that it was in fact a wet road. They were already cold and still had a long way to go.

Two hours later they came to another country road which they followed for a short while to a junction where there was a small hamlet. They would need to get food from somewhere, and their experiences of the Dutch hatred for their occupiers led them both to believe that locals would offer succour. Seeing a small light in one of them Herford cautiously approached and peered through the letter box. All he could see was the illuminated dial of a wireless set playing dance music. He gingerly tapped out a Morse 'V' on the door hoping to illicit a response. He saw a hand quickly reach out and turn the wireless off. He tapped again but no response came. He concluded that he had given someone a terrible fright and decided it was best not to linger.

They continued along the road for another 100 yards until they saw in the distance a roadblock. Either side of the road there seemed to be a large wired-off area. Herford went cautiously ahead, but suddenly heard someone cough alarmingly close. He had almost walked into a manned sentry box which had remained invisible against the background of trees. Luckily the wind and rain had dulled the sentry's alertness, who failed to notice the figure creeping along the grass verge no more than ten yards away.

Cutting their losses they plunged into the woods at the roadside and decided to skirt around the perimeter of the wire. A little further on they emerged from the trees onto an area of sandy waste land and saw several large wireless masts silhouetted against the sky. They reckoned that the fence was surrounding the wireless station and steeled themselves for a lengthy detour. The detour led them into some very thick clinging undergrowth which seemed to grasp and clutch at their soaked clothes. As soon as they cleared it they stopped for a rest, exhausted.

Dan decided it was the right moment to produce his emergency rations, and they both gratefully sank their teeth into the highly concentrated chocolate and dried meat. While they were recovering it was virtually the first opportunity they had had to get to know one another. Dan didn't even know Herford's surname!

They continued uninterrupted for several hours until dawn approached, when they came across a large notice indicating that the area was a German infantry training ground. They continued around the edge until about 7.30 when they were lucky enough to chance upon a deserted cottage, bare of furniture with a stack of straw nearby. They decided to stay there for the daylight hours. The cottage was only 100 yards from a small cross-roads, but there were woods behind into which they could escape if necessary.

They gathered up some sticks and set a small fire in the grate, and even discovered some potatoes in the garden. There were enough for a meal with a few left over to carry with them; the best potatoes they had ever eaten.

After an hour they put out the fire to avoid attracting attention and took it in turns to rest outside in the straw while the other kept lookout. Sleep was almost impossible. Herford carried out several reconnoitres of the surrounding area, checking their position. He had a map which covered the route for part of the journey but couldn't be sure whether they were on the map. They both agreed they would have to travel further south-west before turning south. During the course of the day several German lorries passed by and some troops on bicycles, but they remained unseen. For several hours the sun came out and they managed to rid most of the damp from their clothes.

At 6.15 p.m. they set off again and made good going over a large area of waste land and sparse woodland in the remaining daylight, crossing what appeared to be a large, disused rifle range. Herford was intrigued by a couple of cycle tracks in the sand which seemed to go on and on for miles across this desolate stretch of country.

They calculated they should shortly be reaching the Hoenderlo – Otterlo road. Eventually they did reach a small road, but not the one they thought. They crossed and came upon some very large iron gates at the entrance to a large imposing mansion.They followed the road for some distance in a southerly direction until they arrived at some houses scattered amongst trees. They couldn't get their bearings at all so decided there was nothing for it but to risk asking one of the locals where they were.

Herford cautiously approached one of the houses, but as he came close he heard the heavy thud of field boots and a voice in German as a door opened. He retreated quickly. They continued along the verge for another kilometre, ducking into the ditch several times as cars and trucks passed. Luckily the Germans paid scant regard to the blackout and their headlights gave plenty of warning. However, they had a close shave at one point when Herford saw a notice on the opposite side of the road behind which was a group of what looked like military huts. Without warning a car came around a bend and they flew for cover. The driver seemed to see them, stopped fifty yards down the road, got out of his car and shouted something indecipherable in German. Herford and Dan hugged the ground, praying that he wouldn't come back up the road. At last the man got back in his car and drove on. They breathed sighs of relief, and decided that they had to leave the road straight away and head south-west across country.

They struck out across fields and came to a small farm. There was a dog chained up outside but no humans in evidence. At the next farm Herford peered through a crack in the shuttering and saw a group of German soldiers, obviously on detachment.

Eventually they came across some buildings on the edge of a small village. As they passed the front of a house a woman opened a bedroom window. Herford called out in a stage whisper in English and German, asking the name of the village. The woman was stunned. There was a long pause as she struggled to see who was calling out to her. 'Tommies?' she eventually asked. 'Yes', Herford replied. She then asked why he had spoken in German if he was English. Herford tried to explain but she just said 'Otterlo' and closed the window, obviously very frightened that she was being targeted by German agents.

Herford and Dan were greatly relieved to have chanced upon their half way point so easily. Herford was determined that having coming so far they should get proper directions before striking out on the final leg of their journey. He left Dan in a concealed position at the roadside and proceeded tentatively through the village. He came upon a Red Cross post with loud Dutch voices coming from inside, and quietly tapped on the door. The voices fell silent and a Dutch woman opened a small window and peered out. Herford asked if she spoke English. She looked very frightened and said, 'No. This is only a hospital here,' and promptly shut the window.

On the opposite side of the road was what appeared to be an evacuation centre, again with Dutch voices inside. Herford decided to follow the same procedure and tapped on the door.

A Dutch man came to the door and gave no answer to Herford's question. Instead he looked at his visitor steadily for several seconds, perhaps awaiting some secret sign or signal, then closed the door. Herford and Dan were by now wearing their Airborne waterproof gas cape, as they had observed that so many had been seized and were now being worn by the Germans, they simply looked like German troops with captured waterproofs!

Five minutes later Herford knocked on the same door again. Another man came out, and still saying nothing scrutinised the bedraggled English soldier on his doorstep before shutting the door.

Herford waited, guessing that he was being tested.

Several minutes later a man and a woman emerged from the building and walked down the road, ignoring him completely.

Another few minutes passed before another man emerged. Herford whispered to him. He flashed a torch in his face, looked him up and down, then said, 'Follow me'.

Herford could sense the man was friendly. He told him he was an escaped POW and explained he had a companion waiting along the road. They walked back to where Dan was still hiding and then followed the man to a small wooden hut where five men greeted them warmly.

One of them was a Red Cross worker who had travelled down from Amsterdam that morning with a lorry load of supplies for displaced persons. Herford did not establish exactly who the others were, but did not wish to. All that mattered was the generosity of their hospitality and comradeship. They gave Herford and Dan mugs of hot tea and shared their meagre bread ration. The tea was extremely welcome, but Herford hated being there. If the Germans found these Dutchmen sheltering escaped POWs it meant certain death for them.

The man who had guided them there left for a short while and then returned saying the Germans on the edge of village were just about to move out, but that he would show them the start of the route they must follow to the Rhine. They bid farewell to their hosts and followed the man out into the heavy rain along a muddy track to a main road which they had to cross. There was a stationary German lorry several yards away which appeared to be loading. He told them he would go and distract them and that they should take their chance to cross. With that, he left them. Moments later they heard him laughing and sharing a joke with the soldiers. Herford and Dan slipped across the road and found the track which their guide had told them would lead them the remaining 14 kilometres (8¾ miles) to the Rhine.

In the excitement of their encounter at Otterlo they had had not time to look at their map! They couldn't risk striking a match, so had to recall what they could from memory. They set off at a quick pace, but must have taken a wrong fork because they ended up at another major road, which could only have been the main route from Arnhem to Otterlo. They proceeded cautiously along the verge for some way but there were far too many German vehicles for comfort. At one stage a German soldier riding a bicycle without lights almost knocked them over. Only his whistling gave them enough forewarning to dive into the ditch. Deciding this was far too dangerous they struck out west hoping to find the correct route.

After another kilometre or so they found what they thought was the right track. It was heading due south which was at least the right direction.

By now Dan was suffering from mild dysentery and becoming increasingly exhausted. They stopped for a few minutes every hour during which they dozed fitfully, barely able to keep awake. After one rest they saw flares lighting up the sky to the south and heard salvoes of gunfire and mortars. They were obviously coming close to the front line.

By 3 a.m. they were in a wood and fit to drop. They were sorely tempted to stay where they were for the rest of the day, but decided that another day spent in wet clothes in a sunless wood would only sap them of what little energy they had left. They pushed on until 5 a.m., when they found themselves in a big pine wood, knee deep in undergrowth and then suddenly came upon another major road – the Ede-Arnhem road. On both sides the Germans had dug slit trenches. Tiredness compounded their anxiety. They were desperate for a safe place to conceal themselves for the rest of the day.

Walking south they ran into the tail end of a German vehicle patrol. They waited for it to pass and then crept along the roadside only to come upon some camouflaged German vehicles. There were sounds that the men inside were beginning to wake up. They managed to slip past and into some more woods. They had still been proceeding in single file, but at this stage Dan suggested that as they were likely to encounter many more Germans the closer they came to the front lines, they should walk together in order to attract less attention. Herford agreed that this was the most sensible course of action.

As dawn approached the track took them close to some huts in the woodland. A German soldier came out from one of them about a hundred yards away. He looked closely at them, but seeing the rain he thought better of investigating any further.

As they continued through the trees they came upon more and more huts, from some of which smoke was rising. At the edge of the wood was a wide open area dotted with wrecked RAF gliders shot down in the Airborne landing. They stuck to the edges of the wood and tried to keep out of sight of the huts. However, at one stage the track forced them to walk directly past a front window where a German and a woman were preparing breakfast. They exchanged looks with the occupants who fortunately seemed more interested in their food than in dashing out into the cold wet dawn to tackle two passers-by.

The number of Germans they were encountering was beginning

to feel excessive. They could not rely on their flimsy disguises for much longer so decided to hunt around for a hiding place. They passed a number of other wrecked gliders and finally came upon a thicket of dense oak scrub and undergrowth. When they had crawled into its midst they could not possibly be seen, even from the air. They offered up a prayer of thanks and spent an almost reasonable day sleeping fitfully and absorbing as much of the autumn sunshine as they could. They opened the remains of Dan's rations and ate well, storing up energy for the final three-kilometre trek leg down to the Rhine.

At intervals throughout the day they heard the sound of building hammering and voices coming from the far side of the wood. They also spotted a battery of guns due west. They were clearly in an area of much military activity and decided not to risk making the final approach to the river until it was completely dark.

As twilight gave way to cloudless night and their eyes acclimatised to near blackness, they moved off. They had an unpleasant surprise when they almost crossed paths with a German patrol, but had sufficient time to duck into the trees while they marched past. Desperate not to be captured so close to their objective they decided to stick to the middle of ploughed fields.

Crawling through dry beanplants was back-breaking and noisy, but luckily there was a fair amount of shelling coming from the other side of the river which was occupying the enemy's attention. They only hoped that it stayed to the east and did not switch to their direction.

The shells were landing near enough for them to hear them crashing into the ground followed by the thud of falling earth.

About a kilometre from the river they came to the edges of the Heelsum swamp. From their maps they knew that the area was low lying between two stretches of higher ground. The firmer areas of ground were sticky water-logged turf, the rest was a watery morass. It was uncomfortable to cross but ideal cover. They could hear voices coming from either side, but none in the swamp.

They half crawled, half swam through the seemingly endless banks of reeds and pools, concentrating on nothing except getting to the river. The bombardment seemed to be increasing. The sky was constantly being lit up by flares, forcing them to crawl on their bellies. About 500 yards from the river they stopped in cover just in time to see a German, patrol marching across a marsh. They waited for what seemed like an age before they were happy that the coast was clear. They didn't want to lose it all now.

They followed over the marsh crossing and then headed for the river. Herford was convinced they would find British or Americans almost immediately on the opposite bank. They stopped and packed their boots and heavier items of clothing into their gas capes ready for the swim, but kept on their camouflage smocks.

As they waded waist deep through a flooded area in the direction of Renkum very close to the river, it seemed best to head towards some rising ground to their left. It turned out to be the bank of the river which they were approaching at a very oblique angle.

Not being able to see over the rise of the dyke and down to the river below it was impossible to assess whether this would be a safe place to attempt the swim across. Because the river was swollen and fast moving from days of heavy rain they would be swept a considerable distance downstream. It was therefore critical that they found themselves the clearest possible stretch of bank. They decided that Herford should go ahead and recce while Dan waited.

Herford crept slowly forwards maintaining absolute silence. He looked over the dyke to the Rhine below. He could not see any Germans. He knew that the grey light of dawn could not be far away so it was critical that they make their move. He retraced his steps but Dan was not there. They had agreed that in the event of a separation each should continue. Herford thought that Dan might have gone over to the river bank to look for him there. He climbed back up the dyke, bitterly disappointed that they should have become separated at this vital moment. He dropped down to the river and searched the bank but Dan was nowhere to be seen. Later Herford learned that Dan had gone into the woods on the left and had walked straight into a hornet's nest of Germans on the edge of an area of woodland which extended down to the river bank. At dawn he was recaptured.

Herford looked up and down the bank for his friend in desperation, but there seemed to be nothing to do except go on. Almost opposite on the southern side of the river were some smouldering buildings. The light from the fires lit up the swirling surface of the river. It looked fifty yards across, but was perhaps much more. The water was freezing.

Working quickly he took off his smock and left it on the shoreline as a sign to Dan that he had crossed there. The remainder of his clothes he bundled in his gas cape with his boots, being the heaviest items, at the bottom. He then secured the waterproof 'Airborne bubble' with his boot-laces. This arrangement would allow him to keep his clothes from being soaked as well as providing extra buoyancy.

He waded into the freezing water, the mud oozing around his toes, and uttered a silent prayer. He held the gas cape bubble under his chest and kicked out hard with his legs, knowing that he had to swim as fast as he could to avoid being swept too far downstream into the line of German machine guns. Within moments he was in the fast moving water which carried him along with alarming speed. He used every last ounce of energy, kicking until his legs burned with the effort. The water was so brightly illuminated with flares and exploding shells he felt it must only be moments before the sound of Spandau fire was ringing in his ears. But no fire came; the only sounds were the rush of water breaking around his neck and his heart pounding.

Suddenly he realised that he had cleared the strongest part of the current, and with this realisation came a sudden extra burst of energy which pushed him on to the far side. He grabbed hold of the bank. There was no sloping shoreline here; he had to heave himself out of the water with an almighty effort. He lay at the water's edge catching his breath, wondering what had happened to Dan. He looked along the bank then out across the water but there was no sign.

The relief quickly gave way to the realisation that he was extremely cold. He hastily unwrapped the gas bubble and dressed. He was glad to find his battle dress no damper than it had been on the far side.

His next thoughts were of making contact with someone who would not shoot first and ask questions later, but he had no time to make plans as almost immediately several figures in tin hats appeared at the top of the river bank. Fearing they might shoot, Herford instantly challenged them. The answer came back, 'Sergeant Butcher, 101 US Airborne Division, and who the hell are you?' Herford gave his name, rank and unit and was told to stand still. The patrol approached him with raised rifles and demanded to know what he was doing wandering around in their sector. He explained that he was an escaped POW and that he was looking out for Dan, but they did not appear at all convinced. They marched him off to their HQ, treating him just like a prisoner.

On arrival Herford was warmly received by a young American officer who took down his details and made some telephone calls to corroborate his claims. His bona fides established, he was given some food, his clothes were dried and brushed by a batman and he lay down to sleep in the luxury of dry blankets. The Americans promised to keep a lookout for Dan.

Several hours later Herford was taken to 101 AB Division HQ and then on to 30 Corps HQ where he reported to a young intelligence officer for de-briefing and handed over the lists of POW casualties he had brought with him. The intelligence officer appeared most unimpressed and distinctly bored by the lack of logistical information Herford was able to provide about the other side!

Herford was reunited with his unit later that day where he was warmly welcomed, but whereas the members of the Airborne who had escaped and made it back had been given six weeks leave, he had to struggle to get two!

Johnny Johnston's predictions proved correct. Herford did escape and was duly awarded the Distinguished Service Order. 'What a man!' Johnston wrote to Herford's father, 'They probably let him go to get rid of him! I bet he was the biggest headache they'd had in the POW line for a long time. Your faith in him and our optimism has been more than justified with a bit to spare!'

The lengthy citation in the *London Gazette* of 29 March 1945 gives a more or less accurate account of the achievements which merited this high honour:

'On 23 September 1944, 163 Field Ambulance was moved to area Valburg MR 660690 to act as evacuating medical unit for casualties of 1st Airborne Division from the North bank of the river Neder Rijn in the event of the relief of that Division being successfully accomplished. Reports stated there were 2000 British Casualties in the area north of the river in urgent need of assistance and Medical Supplies. The Medical Personnel of the Division was reduced to 18 officers and 120 Other Ranks.

It was planned that 163 Field Ambulance would accompany a Force across the river on the night 23/24 September and would take across medical personnel and stores, but this plan had to be abandoned owing to the non-availability of sufficient craft.

At 14.30 hours 24 September 1944 Lt Colonel Herford on his own initiative organised a party consisting of one Medical Officer and four Other Ranks and crossed the river to the north bank in a boat loaded with medical equipment. The boat displayed the Red Cross Flag.

Lt Colonel Herford was aware that the north bank was held by the enemy and that all his movements might be under direct observation. On reaching the North bank he ordered his party to remain with the boat while he alone proceeded forward with a view to making contact with the Medical Services of the 1st British Airborne Division or making arrangements with the enemy for the completion of his mission. However, after leaving the bank, he was made prisoner. He requested to be taken to see a Senior German Officer and after some considerable time his request was granted. The result of his interview was that he was permitted to contact the head of German Medical Services in the Arnhem area and arrange for the organisation of a hospital for all British casualties. This hospital was established in Barracks near Apeldoorn. Into this hospital 1500 British casualties were collected and most of the remaining medical personnel of the 1st British Airborne Division were set to work.

Lt Colonel Herford was largely responsible for the organisation of the hospital and treatment of the casualties. When he discovered it was proposed by the Germans to evacuate the serious cases in ordinary freight wagons he protested in the strongest possible terms and succeeded in ensuring the provision of a properly equipped ambulance train. When all the serious cases had been evacuated from Apeldoorn he decided to make his escape. In this he was successful after an arduous and dangerous journey and he returned to our lines,, bringing with him a nominal roll of 1500 British casualties remaining in enemy hands. He was, in all, 26 days within enemy lines.

In carrying out this most dangerous and difficult task Lt Colonel Herford displayed complete disregard for his own personal safety. His unshakeable determination resulted in adequate treatment being afforded to the British Casualties in enemy hands and their evacuation to enemy hospitals under the best possible conditions.

His conduct all through was up to the best traditions of his Corps.'

There is a major inaccuracy in this citation. Herford was not responsible for the 'organisation' of the hospital at Apeldoorn (the administration of which was handled by the Airborne staff), but was entirely responsible for its establishment.

INTO BELSEN

After his escape from Apeldoorn Herford's unit was withdrawn to the port of Antwerp. Fighting would continue in the Arnhem area throughout the winter until a large spring offensive finally broke the German front and brought her into submission.

Herford gratefully accepted his two weeks' leave and sailed home to be greeted by his overjoyed wife and relatives. His phonecall to them just before he left for England was the first news they had had that he was alive.

Two weeks later on 10 November he returned to Antwerp on a dull motionless sea. He had still not received news of Dan McGowan and thought of him constantly. He had been unable to enjoy the triumph of his escape whilst not knowing what had become of his companion. In fact he didn't find out that Dan was a POW until the end of the war.

Herford had comfortable lodgings in a flat in Antwerp, but the relative peace was soon shattered by bombardments from V1 and V2 rockets. Antwerp was a vital supply point for the Allies and it suffered even heavier bombardment than London. On the night of 22 November a V2 exploded in the street outside Herford's flat shaking the whole building, smashing the windows and throwing him out of his bed. It was one of the closest shaves he had during the whole war. Three days previously the welfare centre near which his unit was based was destroyed in an air raid, and in the following weeks they prepared to move to three new locations, but each time the buildings were destroyed.

By mid-December the unit were beginning to feel they had suffered more than their share of bad luck. Herford added to their grumbling by insisting they pack up for another move on a Saturday afternoon, a time when most of them would have been out at the cinema or in a café. As they worked there was an almighty explosion nearby from a lone V2. The news came quickly that the Rex cinema had suffered a direct hit in the middle of the afternoon matinée. There were nearly 200 casualties, most of them British soldiers, and the rescue operation continued for well over 24 hours. Half the men in Herford's unit had intended being there that afternoon. Their narrow escape was the subject of much discussion for several weeks.

The relentless bombardment of Antwerp throughout the winter was especially depressing as the Allied soldiers had entertained high hopes of overrunning Germany before Christmas. Instead it felt as if the pendulum was swinging back the other way. Herford's unit spent most of January, February and March 1945 retrieving and treating the casualties of the air raids. Antwerp was effectively reduced to a dead city, a barren shell of its former self.

Then came the great breakthrough and the crossing of the Rhine at the end of March. A simultaneous thrust by the Second British Army and the Ninth Us Army in the North of Germany, and by the First and Seventh US Armies in the south brought a rapid advance into Germany itself.

Apeldoorn fell to the 5th Canadian Division on 15 April 1945. Herford was immediately anxious to return and find news of his comrades who had remained behind. Despite being told that the road into town was not yet open, he used his well-proven persuasive powers to convince the Canadian soldiers manning the checkpoints en route, of the urgency of his visit. Two days after the town's liberation he returned to the Willhelm III barracks. The buildings were by now largely deserted, the remaining personnel having been moved on into a POW camp in Germany. It was guarded by Canadian soldiers with instructions not to let anyone in, but on hearing his story they allowed him to enter to search for Colonel Warrack's dog-eared diary and any other remaining personal effects. He found the hiding place in the ceiling of Warrack's room, and to his great relief the diary and a little hoard of belongings were still there. These he returned to Warrack's family. He also retrieved a souvenir which could have sentimental value only to himself; the mirror above Warrack's hand wash basin. The same mirror remains on Herford's bathroom wall to this day.

Herford later learned that Warrack had in fact escaped with the help of the Dutch resistance. The morning after Herford and McGowan had got away the Germans issued orders at 8.15 a.m. that with the exception of five MOs, two Padres and twenty RAMC Other Ranks a complete evacuation would take place in two hours. The men deliberately dragged their heels, and by 11.30 Colonel Warrack had disappeared. The Germans were infuriated; they moved all remaining personnel into one block and the guard doubled. On 26 October Major Simon Frazer, now OC, was told that all remaining staff and patients were to be moved to St Joseph's Kreigs-Lazerett. The final evacuation took place that day. All patients were moved including one subaltern who was transported on a bus, whilst receiving a blood transfusion from a Dutch girl (who had been kept in the barracks by German soldiers for their pleasure) and who willingly acted as a donor to keep this man alive.

That afternoon, Herford was delighted to be reunited with Major Simon Fraser, the surgeon with whom he had so carefully cut up the smoked salmon to distribute amongst the wounded soldiers in the Airborne Hospital. The memory of the extreme pangs of hunger suffered by both men, and doubtless the supreme test of will involved in defeating temptation, had etched itself into both their memories. Like many of the bizarre and perverse incidents of war shared by men suddenly and unexpectedly thrown together in deplorable conditions, it formed a deep bond between them.

Herford learned that after his escape, Fraser had continued to work in St Joseph's hospital. The hospital was by now largely evacuated, but still contained twenty wounded British soldiers waiting to be flown home. As Fraser showed him around the crumbling building, Herford realised that in the final months and weeks of German occupation Fraser had performed an heroic task in caring for the sick and wounded with dwindling medical and food supplies. While awaiting rescue the Germans had become increasingly tense and erratic in their moods, and the threat of a bullet in the head from an embittered German soldier hung menacingly over him and his patients until the moment they saw the faces of the first Canadian troops. Ironically, Fraser talked not of his jubilation at being freed, but of his relief in getting hold of Canadian rations. Neither he nor his patients had enjoyed anything approaching a proper meal in months, and while the German soldiers continued to eat well, many of their hospitalised prisoners were in the early stages of starvation.

There is no greater agony for a doctor than to see his patients dying needlessly from lack of the most basic medicine: food. And no greater joy than to see them receiving the nourishment which will save them from the jaws of death. It is a testament to Colonel Herford's level-headedness and unswerving dedication to his work that never once in his diaries does he pour vitriol on those who cruelly treated the prisoners he and Fraser tended in Apeldoorn. His rare ability simply to attend to the task in hand, without being side-tracked by feelings of hatred for an evil enemy, was to prove his greatest asset in the coming weeks. The hardships endured by the prisoners at Apeldoorn would pale into insignificance when compared to those suffered by the inmates of the concentration camp to which he would shortly be posted.

On 27 April Herford's unit was ordered to proceed to the infamous Belsen camp in north-east Germany. At that stage very little was known about the crimes against humanity which had been perpetrated in Hitler's 'dungeons of democracy'. Even the Allied High Command was ignorant of the scale of the atrocities. Until April 1945 only rumours had leaked out, and these were usually dismissed as wildly exaggerated.

On 4 April General Eisenhower followed his troops into Ohdruf, one of the first camps to be taken. He was so shocked by what he saw that he immediately sent photographs of the dead and dying to Churchill. The photographs were circulated to every member of the British cabinet. Within two months the photographic images of Belsen, Auschwitz and Dachau would become eternal symbols of the very depths of human depravity.

Herford ordered his unit to pack and prepare to proceed to Belsen. He travelled ahead of them to the 2nd Army Group Headquarters for briefing. His staff car covered 400 miles in a tortuous overnight journey. Northern Germany was still a chaotic and dangerous place; isolated pockets of resistance meant the route was plagued by interminable detours. The roads were unpredictable, pot-holed and cluttered with army vehicles, bands of miserable displaced persons and abandoned German tanks. Here and there the crack of rifles and thud of mortars was heard. In the distance, like a far-off storm, was the constant rumble of heavy artillery which accompanied the 2nd Army's inexorable advance.

When Herford arrived to receive his orders he was told his unit was being diverted to Neuengamma, a small town almost on the North Sea which was still being held by Nazi troops. It was strongly suspected that a concentration camp would be found there. He was instructed to take over the camp as soon as the Germans had been flushed out. This change of plan saved Herford from witnessing the very first days of the Belsen liberation, but his mission to

Neuengamma was again to place him at tremendous personal risk.

It was now 2 May. Still proceeding ahead of his unit, Herford drove north-west to Geestbacht, a suburb of Hamburg and the location of Field Marshall Montgomery's Headquarters. There he reported to Brigadier Wimsey of 158 Brigade and successfully negotiated the loan of a jeep and the services of a medical orderly. From Hamburg they drove the 30 miles north-west along the coast towards Neuengamma under the white flag. This was a necessary precaution in territory still hotly disputed by ad-hoc groups of stubborn Nazi troops.

As they neared their destination they came across a British Bren patrol returning to base after having come under heavy fire. Herford was warned that advancing further would involve serious risk, and was strongly advised to turn back. They had reached the front line. The most sensible course would have been to wait for the resistance to be crushed and to follow the Allied troops into Neuengamma.

Having heard some of the first reports which had emerged from Belsen, Herford was in no mood for retreating. He had determined that nothing would prevent him from getting to the wretched inmates of the camp as soon as possible. But rather than risk the life of the orderly he decided to proceed alone, on foot.

He had gone only a short distance when he came upon a group of German soldiers and demanded to see their senior officer. It was an outrageous risk. Soldiers in the last throes of battle are notoriously ruthless. He had no protection other than a square of white cloth and a quick wit. Fortunately, his luck held. Even in the face of defeat, the soldiers remained sufficiently honourable to take him blindfolded to their Commander.

The Commander was an ex-Corvette captain, a rabid Nazi, fanatically determined to resist to the last. The command structure in the area had completely broken down, but his troops were continuing to fight in battle-groups, driven on by the obstinacy of their leader.

On meeting Herford, he immediately told him that Hitler was as great a man as Jesus Christ!

Herford demanded access to the Neuengamma camp, but the Commander informed him that it had already been evacuated. This was not the safest of situations in which to threaten an enemy officer, but nonetheless Herford warned him that if he was later discovered to have lied, he and his fellow officers would be held personally responsible. Before returning to his jeep, he also told the Commander details of the initial reports from Belsen. Apparently he was visibly shocked. Even among the German officer class, it appears that ignorance was rife.

It was later to emerge that Neuengamma had been the scene of crimes against humanity as bad as any of those throughout the war. In total 90,000 people passed through its gates, 40,000 of whom died there, the victims of unspeakable brutality. Amongst the most unfortunate of the inmates were a group of twenty French and Russian Jewish children, who in February 1945 were selected by Dr Heissmeyer, a Berlin physician, for medical 'research' into tuberculosis. During the following three months Heissmeyer made frequent visits to Neuengamma during which he injected his unsuspecting victims with TB bacteria. While the experiments were being carried out the children were given sweets, and toys to play with.

As the Allies closed in, orders were given by SS General Pohl that the children should be taken to Bullenhausendamn, a satellite camp, and executed, so that evidence of the research would be destroyed. The children and four adult prisoners (two Dutch and two French doctors who had assumed the role of nurses), were accompanied to Bullenhausendamn by Dr Trzerbinski, one of the camp doctors. The prisoners were taken to a cellar. The adults were removed to another room and hanged. In an uncharacteristic act of 'mercy' Trzerbinski injected the children with morphia so that they would be unconscious when hanged. Their executioner was Johann Frahm. Ropes were placed around their necks, and in Frahm's own words, 'like pictures they were hanged on hooks on the walls.'

The other inmates were no less unfortunate. A week before Herford's visit to the area they were loaded onto two ships and three barges which were towed towards Norway, in the certain expectation that they would be mistaken for German industrial vessels and sunk by Allied planes. The ships were duly attacked and the barges set on fire. One of the barges drifted back to the shore near Lubeck carrying 400 survivors. As they clambered ashore German soldiers ruthlessly gunned them down in the sand. None survived.

Herford returned from this fruitless meeting to Geestbacht. At the end of his journey he was an unwitting witness to an historical event. As he was walking back to his quarters he noticed a group of very Senior German officers being guided to Monty's HQ under escort. It was the armistice party of the German army, desperate to surrender to the British rather than the Russians, who were pressing them hard.

It was now 3 May. Herford was ordered to spend the day locating suitable sites for POW camps and hospitals at Lubeck, but the available resources were pitifully inadequate. On that day many tens of thousands of German soldiers poured across the Allied lines. It was a sea of grey uniforms, as far as the eye could see. Such large numbers of prisoners were quite unexpected. There had been no time to prepare adequate facilities, with the result that they did not experience the most humane treatment. They were herded into hastily erected barbed wire compounds with insufficient shelter and facilities. Many of the prisoners were young teenagers, ill-equipped for war, conscripted by an increasingly desperate and callous regime which proved itself more than willing to send them to their deaths.

Herford and his unit entered Belsen on 4 May, nine days after its liberation. The intervening time had done little to ameliorate the suffering of the survivors, who were still dying at a rate of sixty per day. Thousands of stinking, emaciated corpses were still strewn everywhere, and were gradually being heaped into piles for burial in huge grave pits.

Belsen had no gas chambers, but 35,000 corpses were counted, and of the 30,000 survivors, seventy percent required hospitalisation. The chief causes of death were starvation and disease, mainly typhus, tuberculosis and dysentery. All were as a result of the most shocking wilful neglect.

Like many who were unfortunate enough to witness such sights, Herford experienced difficulty in translating the full enormity of what he saw into words. His diary entries are brief but poignant:

'Although No 32 Casualty Clearing Station and No 11 Light Field Ambulance had done magnificent work there in the previous ten days, it was still a distressing sight that can never be erased from the memory. Piles of corpses lay everywhere, naked and emaciated. Huge grave pits were filled with thousands of bodies. Sub-human creatures prowled about apathetically with expressionless eyes. The huts were so crowded that it was impossible to tell the living from the dead. Yet miraculously, many had retained their magnanimity and humanity.'

Fortunately for the survivors, Herford was a consummate administrator as well as doctor. Whilst many exposed to such conditions would have failed, he and his unit were able to get on with bringing many back from the brink of death. The job of the medical teams in the newly liberated Belsen was harrowing, and many harsh decisions had to be made. British doctors were forced to move among the survivors and mark the foreheads of those likely to survive with a red cross. It was a heart-rending task, but absolutely necessary.

The eye-witness accounts from Belsen and other camps finally convinced the soldiers and any remaining doubters at home of the justice of their cause. Peter Coombes, one of the first soldiers into the camp wrote:

'I have never seen people looking so ill, so wretched and so near death. Belsen is a living death, an example of Nazi methods, the best indictment of their government one could ever find, and if it is necessary, an undoubted answer to those who want to know what we have been fighting for. One feeble movement of the hand in salutation to us from these people is also an answer, for our coming has saved thousands in this camp alone, but for many it is too late.'

In the first days after liberation soldiers and nurses had acted hastily, giving food to whoever they could. But the richness of the British army rations: tinned meat, oatmeal, dried milk-powder, sugar and salt was too much for those in the final stages of starvation. Tragically many died as a result of this kindness.

The inhumanity of the camp guards was well documented by the survivors. The ethic according to which they operated was brutal and straightforward: 'Break the body: break the spirit: break the heart.' Amongst those who did not break, and who owed their lives to the British medical teams, was Fania Fenlon. Even in the first week of April she and the other inmates still had no idea when liberation would come. At that time she wrote:

'Hastily built to last a few months, our temporary barracks were half-collapsing; the planks were coming apart. Looking at the damage, a scornful SS man said, speaking of us, the Jews, 'They rot everything, even wood.'
It was true, we were rotting, but it was hardly our fault

214

as their presence alone would taint the healthiest beings.

A few days later, I too had typhus. My last vision as a healthy person was of the women of the camp, like everyone else, outside, naked, lining up to wash our dresses and underclothes in the thin trickle of water from the pierced pipe. On the other side of the wire, the men were doing the same; we were like two troops of cattle at the half-empty trough of an abattoir.

Now the illness took me over entirely; my head was bursting, my body trembling, my intestines and stomach were agony, and I had the most abominable dysentery. I was just a sick animal lying in its own excrement.

From April 8 everything around me became nightmarish . . . No one visited us any more, not even the SS. They'd turned off the water.'

For five days before liberation there had been no water at all. The hut lavatories had been out of use for a long time before that. Most inmates, too ill or weak to move, performed their bodily functions where they lay. The floors and bunks of the huts were covered in human excreta. The living, dead and dying lay in lice infested heaps, barely distinguishable from one another. Conditions for the spread of disease could not have been worse; only feeble attempts had been made in the last days before the Allies arrived to remove corpses from the living accommodation. In one hut, which was close to a pile of corpses awaiting disposal in a mass grave, there were dead women lying in the passage; in one room leading out of the passage there were so many bodies that it was impossible to squeeze in even one more.

The extremes of hunger even drove some poor inmates to cannibalism. One British Intelligence Officer who was at Belsen at the same time as Herford gave evidence at the trial of the Commandant,

Joseph Kramer, that as many as one in ten of the bodies his staff cleared away had a piece of flesh cut from the thigh. At first he assumed they were close gun shot wounds. Later he witnessed at first hand a starving mortuary attendant whipping out a knife and cutting a chunk of flesh from a corpse. He concluded his testimony to the court thus: 'I leave it to your imagination to realise what state the prisoners were reduced, for men to risk eating bits of flesh cut from black corpses.'

In such conditions Herford and his team were forced to work and bring some semblance of order. The mental discipline required to keep a level head when dealing with prisoners who were not only physically, but often mentally sick, was tremendous. In one recorded instance a woman approached a British soldier begging for milk for her baby. The soldier took the baby and found that it had been dead for many days. The woman continued begging, so out of compassion he placed some milk on the dead baby's lips. The mother then started to croon with joy and carried the baby away in triumph. She stumbled and fell dead in a few yards.

As a German speaker, Herford heard first hand from his patients, many of them German 'undesirables', gypsies, homosexuals and 'enemies of the state', the full extent of the atrocities. It is not surprising, therefore, that he and many of his colleagues choose to speak little of the things that disturbed them most. Frustrating as such reticence may be to the researcher of history, it is a profound mark of the humility of those who were present, that they will not presume to communicate the enormity of what they witnessed through the inadequate testimony of an individual voice.

Colonel T M Backhouse, the chief prosecutor at the Belsen trials had no choice but to attempt a description of conditions discovered in the camp. He opened his case with a film taken shortly after the arrival of the British Army. He told the court:

'This film will give you some idea of the conditions and the degradation to which the human mind can descend. You will see thousands of corpses lying about and the condition of the bodies. You will also see the well-fed condition of the SS who were stationed there. You will see people fishing for water with tins in a small tank. What you will not see is that the water was foul and there were dead bodies in it. That was all the water that was available to drink. You will see the dead; you will see the living; and you will actually see the dying. What the film cannot give you is the abominable smell, the filth and squalor of the whole place which stank to high heaven.'

At the time when these trials were taking place in Luneberg, the same film was shown to a local audience of Germans. Apparently it was the source of some amusement. Many of them presumed it to be British propaganda.

Herford spent a frantic week in Belsen – probably the longest of his life – during which time his unit helped save the lives of thousands of Hitler's victims, and ease the passing of countless others. The logistical problems were enormous, but within a few weeks the camps had been cleared, and the survivors requiring treatment transferred to military hospitals. 8 May 1945 was Victory in Europe day, but Herford was scarcely aware of the German surrender, so involved was his unit in coping with the aftermath of the Belsen tragedy.

All that remained of Belsen was its name, which quickly passed into the language as synonymous with inhumanity and evil.

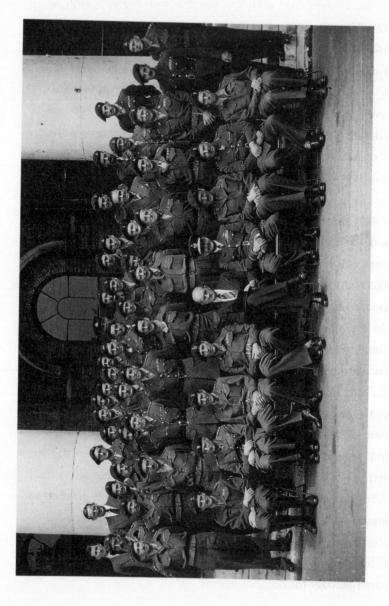

After the war. Martin Herford (bottom right) with comrades in the Airborne Division.

EPILOGUE

The end of war in Europe brought the end of Herford's military ambitions. Fellow officers tried to persuade him that with his distinguished record he continue to build on his achievements with a fulfilling career in the regular army. His bravery and sense of duty were unquestionable and his achievements had been richly rewarded with a row of medals; but he strongly felt that now war was over his medical training could best be used in service to the civilian public.

Like many servicemen anxious for release back to their wives and families Herford had a long wait for his demobilisation. On 1 June his unit was moved to Goslar in the Herz mountains where they became responsible for the provision of food and medical supplies to some 40,000 displaced persons and German wounded in an area 100 miles square. It was a curious time. The fight had completely gone out of the German people. Many of them assumed that Germany as a nation would never exist again. And despite the atrocities for which the Nazis were responsible, Herford remarked that neither he nor his men ever felt or displayed anger or animosity towards the people they were now helping. Such was the sense of relief that six years of battle were over; there was no room for triumphalism.

On 17 August 1945, three days after the end of war in the Far East, Herford was promoted to Colonel Assistant Director Medical Services 5th British Infantry Division in Brunswick. He was gratified to have received the appointment, but it did not sway his resolve to leave. He applied for a Rockefeller Fellowship to study Occupational Hygiene at Harvard which he was granted on 5 October, but he had to wait until January for his final release.

Happily married to Mary for over forty years, he became the proud father of four daughters. Still very much in active retirement in Cornwall, at the age of eighty-six, Herford manages a small farm and holiday cottages business with the same energy that he brought to bear in his Field Ambulance Unit.

He is a formidable man and in war and peace served selflessly as a soldier for justice.